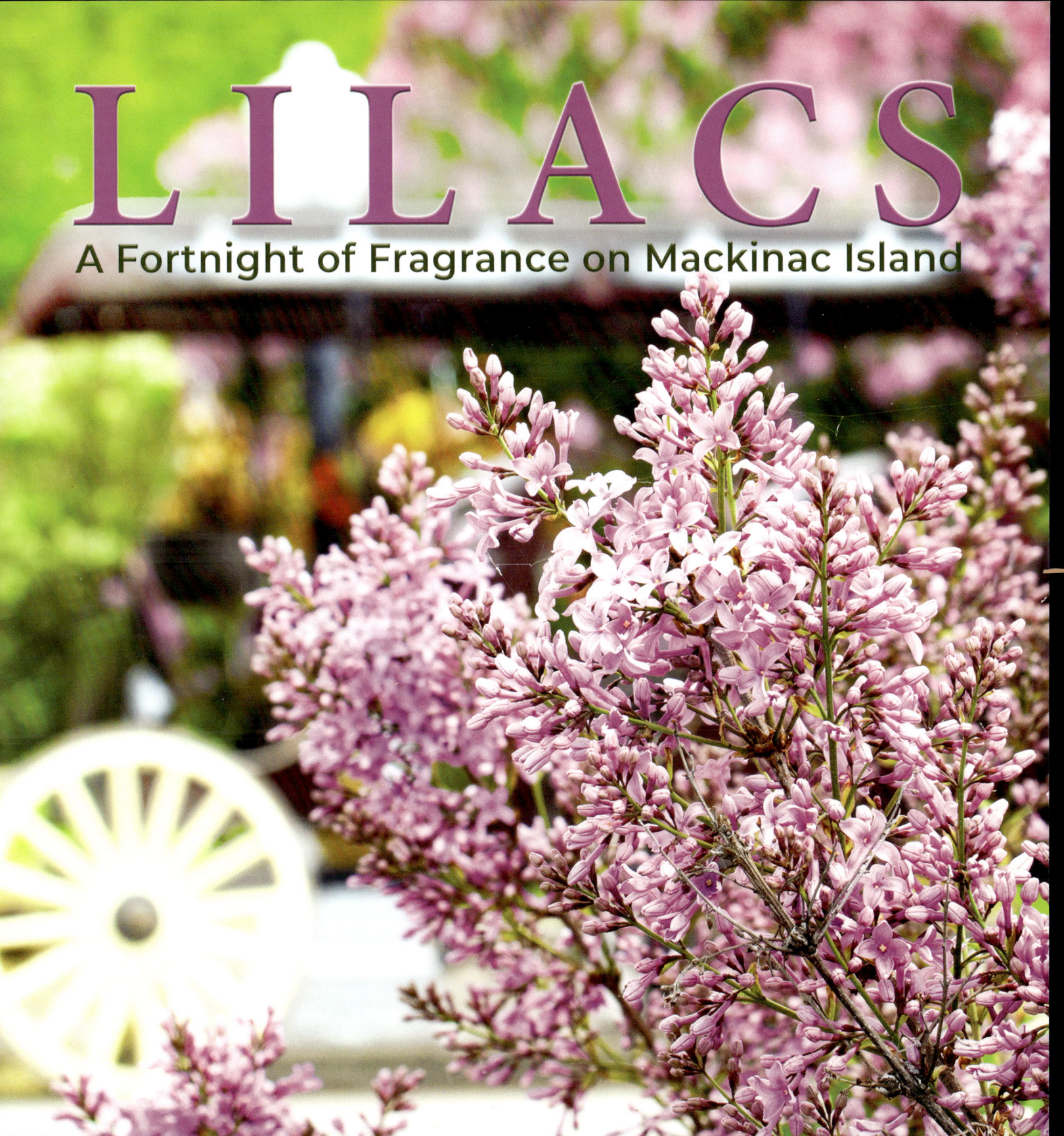

LILACS
A Fortnight of Fragrance on Mackinac Island

Jennifer Wohletz

LILACS
A Fortnight of Fragrance on Mackinac Island

*Harry,
Many thanks for your many kindnesses —
Best Wishes
Jeff*

by SUE ALLEN
with JEFF YOUNG

photography by JENNIFER WOHLETZ
with guest contributors

published by MACKINAC MEMORIES LLC

LILACS
A Fortnight of Fragrance on Mackinac Island

by Sue Allen with Jeff Young

Foreword by Jeff Young

Preface by Bob Benser, president,
Mackinac Island Tourism Bureau

Photography by Jennifer Wohletz

Edited & Designed by Jennifer Wohletz

Contributing Artists, Photographers & Poets:
Sue Allen, Kevin Barton, Jim Bogan, Joe Cilluffo, Stephanie Crane, Maeve Croghan, JC Demers, Kate Dupre, Jim Lenfestey, Nancy May, Diane Neyer, Phillip Rice, Joanne Ripple, Allison Sehoyan, Noel Skiba, Jimmy Taylor, Betty Bea Washburn, Dan Wohletz, Natalia Wohletz, Richard Wolfgang, Sara Wright, Glen Young and Jan Young

Published by Mackinac Memories, llc.
mackinacislandmemories.com/books
mackinacmemoriesllc@gmail.com

Proceeds from this book will benefit the
Mackinac Island Lilac Preservation Fund
Mackinac Island Toursim Bureau
mackinacisland.org | info@mackinacisland.org

No part of this book may be copied or reproduced without written consent of The Mackinac Island Tourism Bureau and Mackinac Memories, llc. Designed in Michigan. Printed in Canada.
First Printing: April 2021

ISBN: 978-0-9973847-7-2

This book is dedicated to the lilacs of Mackinac Island and all those who cherish and protect them.

Dan Wohletz

TABLE OF CONTENTS

Preface
9

Introduction
18

The Old Giants
23

The Gilded Age
45

Foreword
12

LILACS - A Fortnight of Fragrance

The Baby Boomers 65

The 21st Century 79

The Lilac Festival 125

The Future of Mackinac Island's Lilacs 143

About 150

Bibliography 152

PREFACE

by Bob Benser, president
Mackinac Island Tourism Bureau

Lilac Preservation Fund: Sustaining Iconic Shrubs for Future Generations to Enjoy

In the early weeks of June, lilacs on Mackinac launch a fortnight of fragrance. These lush blossoms cast a spell on the little isle, perfuming the misty air for approximately two weeks. So strong is their scent, that people have reported smelling island lilacs from ferries as far as a mile offshore when the wind is right. For centuries, residents and visitors have cherished these iconic blossoms. As home to thousands of lilac plants representing more than 300 kinds, there are few spots outside the island's forests where lilacs aren't found.

Although hardy and prolific, these plants cannot be taken for granted and require protection. In that spirit, the Mackinac Island Tourism Bureau has established the new Mackinac Island Lilac Preservation Fund. All proceeds from this book will go into the fund with the mission of ensuring their protection and care, and expanding their diversity for generations to come.

When people think of Mackinac, they think horses, history, fudge and lilacs. These marvelous plants are an integral part of the island's beauty and economy. The preservation fund will help ensure there will be lilacs blooming here long after we're gone. Thank you for purchasing this book. Your contribution will help sustain Mackinac's lilacs so your grandchildren and theirs may come and enjoy them too.

Facing page: Horses, history and lilacs are interwoven into Mackinac Island's fabric. Here a 'Pocahontas' (Syringa x hyacinthiflora) lilac at the State Harbor delights passers-by.

Beaded dew glosses your petals
Tiny perfumed palms release
The scent of lilacs

Jennifer Wohletz

FOREWORD

by Jeff Young, master gardener
Vermont Master Gardener Class of 2005
St Albans Vermont 2020

Enjoy the Beauty, Richness of Mackinac's Unique Botanical World

Lilacs are memory stimulators that often remind us of someone who has that special connection to the world of plants and gardening. Growing up on my grandparents farm in rural Maine, I remember my grandmother, Gertrude Folsom Young. She was an extraordinary gardener and had an amazing connection to the natural world. It wasn't until much later and after she was long gone that I grew to appreciate that connection and her big old lilac hedge down by the barn. I can still smell the many lilac stems she cut and presented on the dining room table.

Whenever I visit Mackinac Island in June, fond memories of my grandmother come flooding back as I inhale the sweet fragrance of hundreds of different lilacs blooming. On Mackinac, beautiful ornamental lilacs abound, woven into the very fabric of the island. They're not just in a park or special area, but also at homes, inns, and along streets, little lanes and alleys. You can enjoy them almost anywhere you go on the island. They are a mystery waiting to unfold.

Mackinac Island's community members celebrate these iconic blooms during the Mackinac Island Lilac Festival each year. I made my first visit to the island in 2005 to serve as the festival's lilac expert.

continued on next page

Allison Sehoyan

Smell the Blooms, Let Your Senses Take Over

continued from the previous page

I have enjoyed sharing my knowledge with visitors and teaching the art of lilac planting, pruning and maintenance with island horticulturists and Mackinac Island State Park employees.

My journey into lilacs started with the purchase of several lilac shrubs and planting them in my front yard in Vermont. A search for how to care for them led me to the International Lilac Society where I met some of the nicest plant people in the United States and Canada, and realized that I knew little about lilacs (or plants, for that matter). Many of these experts took time and patience to help me in my new adventure into horticulture.

After the convention, I earned my Master Gardener certification by working in a local park, then served as a lilac expert for the Shelburne Museum in Shelburne, Vermont, an instructor at the University of Vermont Horticulture Research and Education Center, and presenter on lilacs throughout the U.S. and Canada. I have returned to Mackinac in June for the past 15 years to lead walk-and-talks, perform presentations about lilacs and demonstrate pruning and planting techniques during the Lilac Festival. I hope this book brings my lilac adventure full circle by passing on my awe and joy of this small, but unique, part of the horticultural world.

While you may be curious about the names and varieties of each plant you see on Mackinac Island, I recommend letting your senses take over and simply enjoy the beauty and the richness of this unique botanical world. May this book help you remember your favorite island places and say, "I was there and that lilac smelled wonderful."

Jewels of early June
Perfuming our yard
Purple, white, magenta

INTRODUCTION

Lilacs: A Mystery Waiting to Unfold

Residents and visitors to Mackinac Island have long loved their lilacs. For a few weeks in June, the fragrance of these lush colorful blossoms stirs our senses, and the romance begins again. It isn't only on Mackinac – people around the world love them too, and have for centuries. They've inspired artists, poets, gardeners and entire communities. In North America, many festivals are dedicated to lilacs. On Mackinac Island, the Lilac Festival began in 1948, making it one of the oldest festivals of its kind in this country, and it has continued for more than seven decades. Poet Robert Nelson called it the "purple canopy," yet these flowers come in a rainbow palette of lavenders, pinks, blues and whites in all shapes and sizes, from the tall old giants to delicate little 'Tinkerbelle's'.

Although not native to the U.S. – they are originally from eastern Europe and Asia – lilacs have adapted remarkably well to Mackinac. The island conditions, with moist cool weather, lake breezes, long winters and limestone soil, are perfect for lilacs. The iconic blossoms grow all over the island, from back alleys to the Grand Hotel's hillside to entire hedges at British Landing. Their crown jewel is Marquette Park, with approximately 115 plants of about 75 varieties. Most new landscapes, whether at a hotel, bed and breakfast or a home, include at least one lilac. Bay View Bed & Breakfast owner Lydia Yoder planted a hedge of lilacs (see photo) 22 years ago, just before the birth of her daughter, Sarah Bailey Yoder. The hardy, late blooming variety thrives in the inn's sunny side yard. "It's been wonderful to watch Sarah grow right along with the lilac," says Lydia. Having established themselves so thoroughly in the soil of Mackinac and the souls of its people, lilacs are now linked with the island as much as horses and history. And our love for them is here to stay.

Jennifer Wohletz

Tender young blossoms
Watch the old sentry
On another shore

Dan Wohletz

THE OLD GIANTS

Lilacs Defy Longevity, Growth Expectations Around the Globe

During lilac time, a canopy of color rises as high as 18 feet on Mackinac's oldest lilacs. The abundance of flowers, and the sheer height and size of their trunks is truly unique. Like the trees in a Tolkien novel, the branches of these old giants twist and turn, taking the trenched bark on a roller coaster ride.

Here and there along the gnarled limbs, bark circles around holes, giving the impression of a carved animal with deep-set eyes. Nowhere else on the planet can you find such architecture as this in a lilac: botanists and lilac enthusiasts marvel at them, but none can explain why a plant that began as a common lilac shrub grew into such an immense and long-lived tree.

A scattering of these very old specimens grow in a few downtown locations, mainly in the Mission District and at the Astor House on Cadotte Avenue. About 10 years ago, a botanist took borings from their trunks to determine their age. Based on ring counts of the extracted samples, he concluded they were 118 years old – but that would only be the age of the plant's second growth, since the stems from which the samples were taken grew out of a previous stem that had died more than a century earlier. Since the original stem probably lived about 100 years, this means the tree is more than 200 years old.

The best example of this is the lilac in front of the Harbour View Inn on the east side. You can see the old trunk laying on its side and the current trunk growing out of it. Both trunks are over 2 1/2 feet in diameter. There is documentation that this lilac was planted in the early 19th Century.

continued on page 29

Jennifer Wohletz

Jennifer Wohletz

The oldest known lilacs can be found in front of the Harbour View Inn and tucked in a cedar hedge across Main Street from the inn in the Mission District. "Having them here is an honor, but it's also a responsibility that we take very personally," says Michelle Dean, Harbour View's general manager. "They are so old, and we worry when the wind is strong and what may happen to them during the winter." The lilac trees there could date back to the time its original owner, Magdelaine La Framboise, lived there from 1822 to 1846. She was a talented business woman who ran a fur-trading business, and her home – now the inn – was a salon in her day.

Jennifer Wohletz

Our Better Monuments Are Found in the Old Giants

by Glen Young

In mid-day warmth, cormorants overhead,
the white fence and the hour's soundtrack

a bird's call behind the lake's steady undulation.
In the quiet of the season's rhythm,
only the labs and me moving in the street,

I paused near the familiar yard, as one
and then another of the old giants,

the better monuments--these lilacs--
certainly the better testaments here,
sighed, their fragrant slender touch soft

against a neighbor's clapboards and sills,
keeping pace in bud and molt and repeat.

Never did any shrine endure like these old giants,
rooted here in flower and then fall.
Certainly no marble artists' molds

sign any languages more fragrant,
letter by letter or sound by sound,

than these wild colors, these holy perfumes.
No granite or bronze can ever outdo
this alchemy of chance and limestone,

these branches, the veiny hands
of visible gods, holding cups of sunlight.

Jennifer Wohletz

Jennifer Wohletz

Ancient Sentinels Witness Island Growth Over Two Centuries

continued from page 23

These ancient sentinels have seen the movement of Mackinac through the years. They were there when Madame La Framboise, original owner of the house that is now the inn, had them planted in the 1820s. They were there when Marquette Park, once a vegetable garden for soldiers at the fort, was developed into a park, and the statue of Pere Marquette placed in its center in 1909 along with a number of lilacs. They witnessed the first Lilac Day Parade in 1949, heard the marching feet and trumpets, the hooves of horses, the beat of the drums.

The huge lilac towering over the yard at the Mackinac Island Carriage Tour property (left) on Cadotte Avenue has watched countless numbers of bikers and carriage horses pass by as they tour the island. It's estimated to be between 50-100 years old. Over the years they have silently watched the demise of many of their sister lilacs, taken by ice, development and old age, and the addition of new and exotic cultivars.

Dan Wohletz

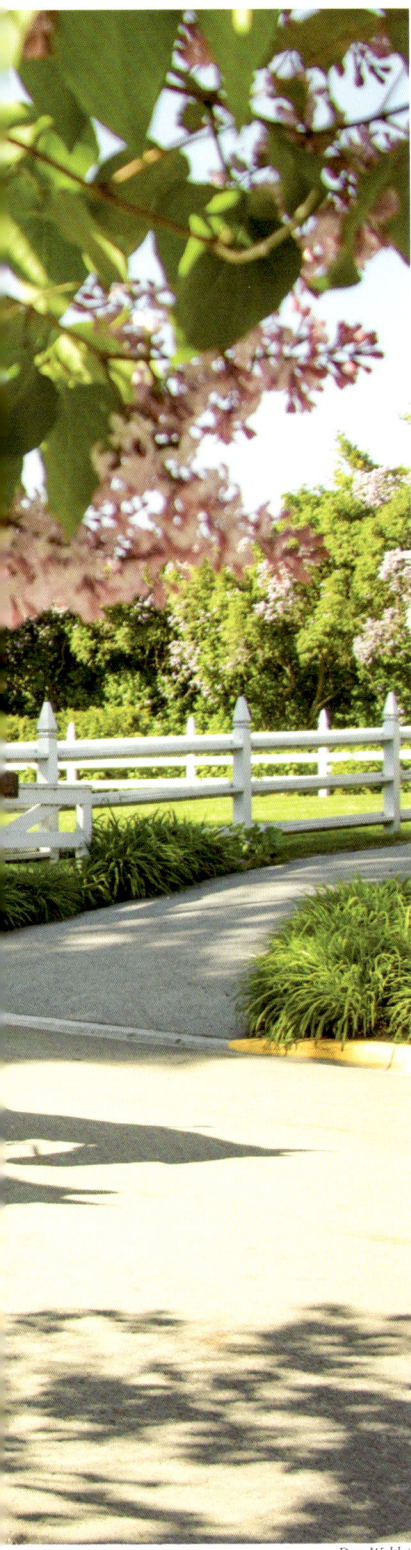

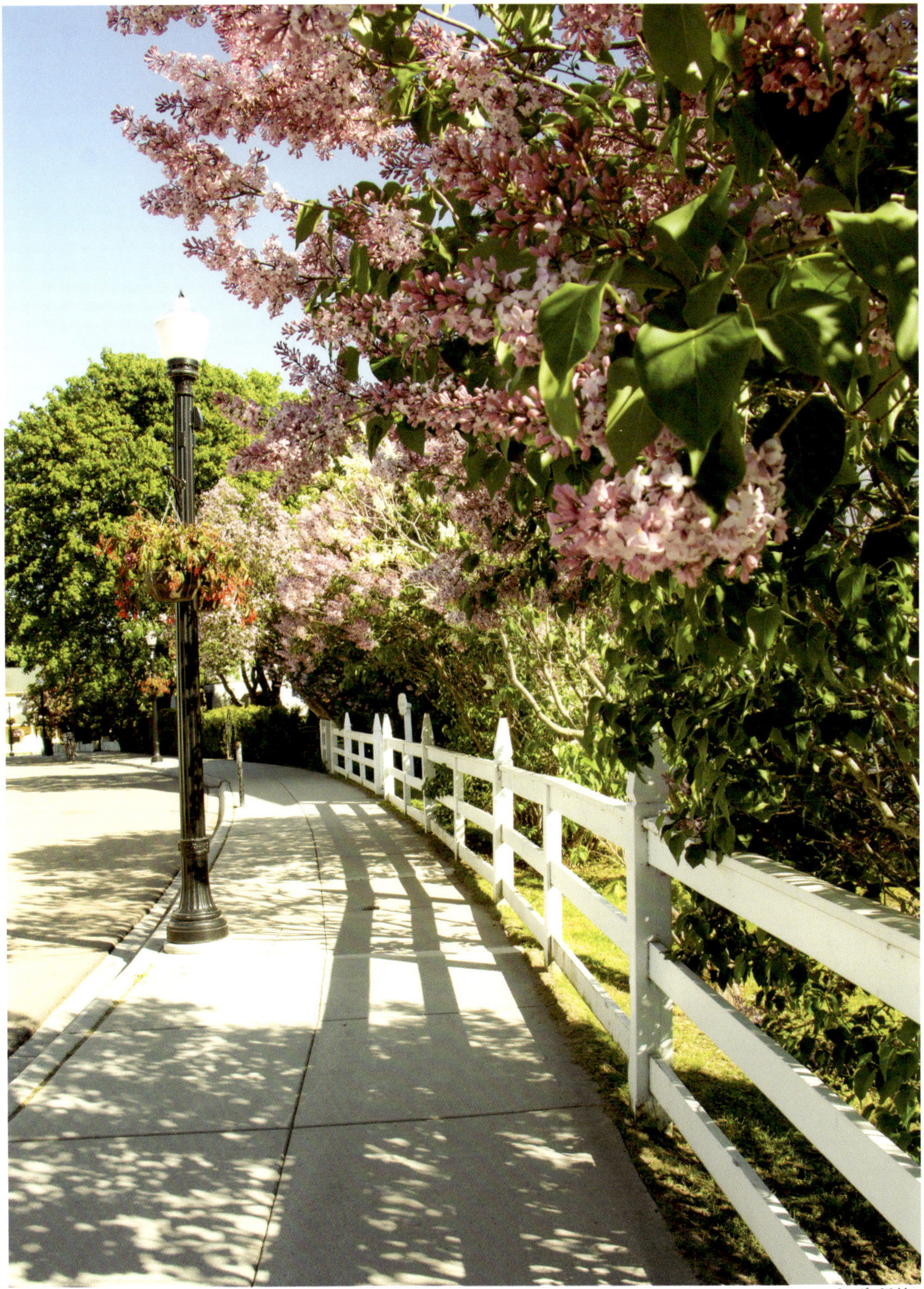
Jennifer Wohletz

Lilacs wave in the breeze as a carriage passes by on Cadotte Avenue.

Jennifer Wohletz

Left: This magnificent lilac tree began as a shrub. Now it's up to the rooftop of the Grand Cottage, the former home of William Backhouse Astor and one of the oldest wooden structures on Cadotte Avenue. Astor ran the American Fur Company out of the building in the early 1800s. Above: Twisted by time and in need of support, the current tree is the second growth and came after the first growth which is evidenced by the old stump. This is called "stem-on-stem." Islanders will do just about anything to save the life of their lilacs, including using rocks, fence posts, two-by-fours and bungie cords to hold up the trunk and/or branches – showing a reverence for the plant.

Jennifer Wohletz

Jennifer Wohletz

Right: This cottage in the Mission District is hidden behind a screen of purple. "From my earliest memory, the fragrance of the lilac trees in my grandmother's yard was pervasive. Since her side yard was so big, we have many varieties with lovely gradations of color. No doubt, one of the most special things about Mackinac Island is the lilac trees," says Elizabeth McDonnell Fox, daughter of Kathleen Dennany McDonnell and granddaughter of Loretta Murray Dennany. Above: The picket fence at the Jacob Wendell Cottage serves a dual purpose as a lilac support.

Jennifer Wohletz

Jennifer Wohletz

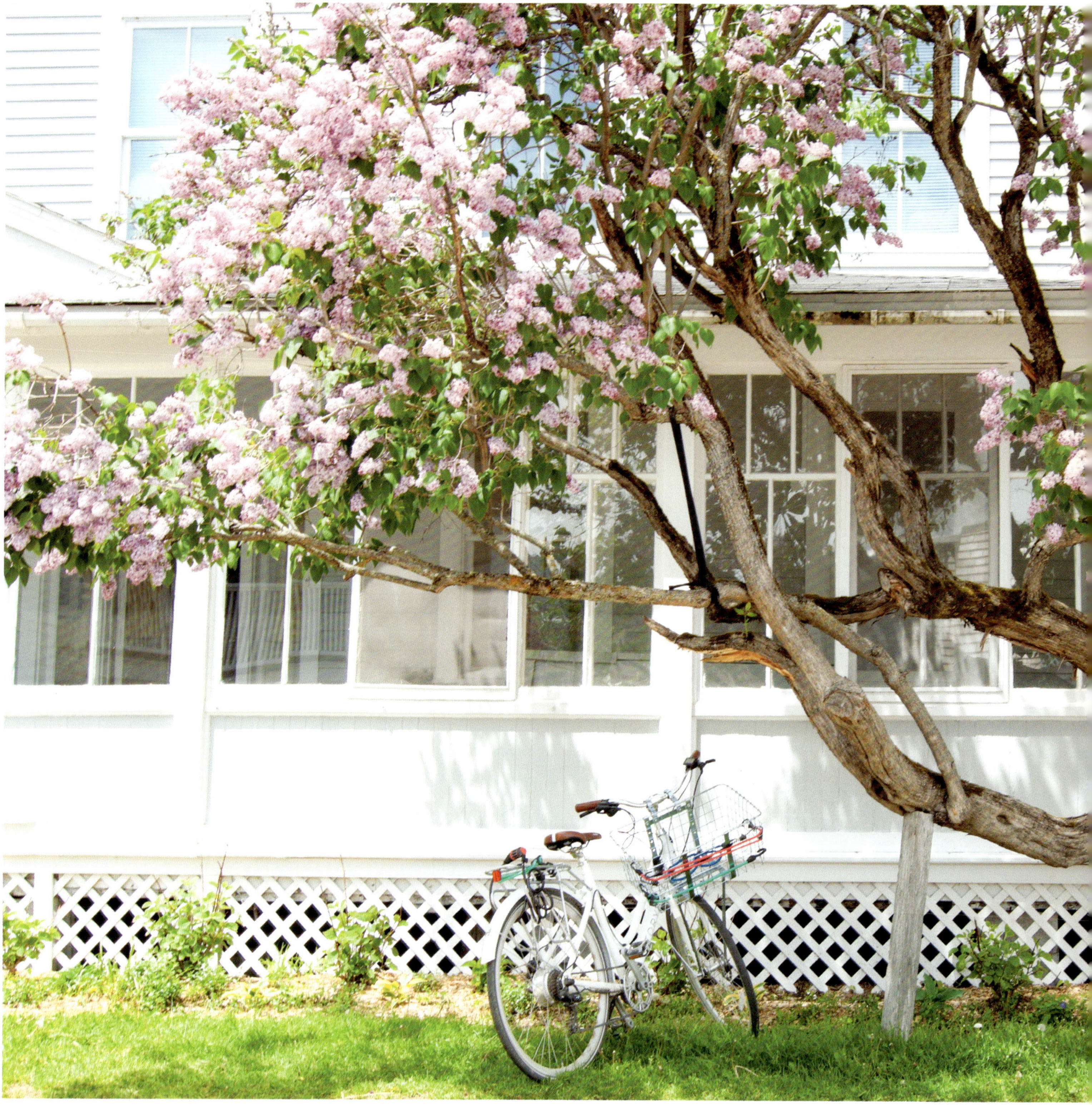

Left: Islanders love their lilacs, and make great efforts to sustain them. A piece of lumber gives a bit of support to this "old giant" in front of Mackinac Island Carriage Tours Lennox Office. Above: Lilacs frame views of a taxi and tour carriages on Market Street.

Jennifer Wohletz

Above & right: A beautiful old lilac shrub and tree near the Boardwalk are in great shape despite the harsh lake conditions. Many of the old trees on Mackinac Island had their suckers cut – like this tree. Facing page: This twisty twirly trunk comes from the wind "All trees have a slight twist from the right; the reason is so they can diffuse the wind, the tree will twist back and forth to diffuse the energy. This lilac is one of those beautiful quirks of nature you find on the island," explains lilac expert Jeff Young.

Jennifer Wohletz

Jennifer Wohletz

Fragrant immigrants, Lilacs Traveled Here from Distant Shores

How did lilacs get to Mackinac Island? Sturdy and strong, lilacs make ideal travelers. And travel they have, making their way over centuries, thousands of miles of land and sea, from the mountainous regions of Eastern Europe to the American colonies. The *Syringa vulgaris* – the common lilac – found in more than 250-300 cultivars on Mackinac Island, is not native to the U.S. These lilacs came to American shores as immigrants in the luggage of new settlers, probably the Dutch and French who were so fond of lilacs. Both plant and people thrived in their new surroundings. Lilacs took to the cold climate. Easily grown from suckers and seeds, the fragrant and beloved lilac spread quickly through the northern colonies and territories.

Horticulturists think that the first lilacs were brought to Mackinac in the early 1800s. One of the earliest records was a phrase in David Thoreau's journal when he visited the island in 1861 that said, "Apple in bloom and lilacs." Some speculate the Hubbard family, who were farmers from New Hampshire, where lilacs were so numerous they became the state flower, brought the first lilacs. They planted them on their new farm on the west side of the island. Today this area is called Hubbard's Annex.

No matter how lilacs arrived, they have thrived, especially the old giants. What began as shrubs and kept growing, defying the longevity and growth expectations of lilacs around the globe, have earned the reputation as the largest lilacs anywhere. Though their crooked posture cannot be straightened, nor their gnarled boughs untangled, these old giants hold their heads high, presenting a singular display of flowers each June. Their secrets are locked in their genes, and we are the fortunate recipients of their long-lasting beauty.

Jennifer Wohletz

Jennifer Wohletz

Jennifer Wohletz

Above: A lilac hedge featuring three varieties in the backyard of a Hubbard's Annex cottage. On the left is a Spaeth, which would have been the No. 1 choice for a dark lilac in the 1920s-40s. The light pink lilac is most likely a Sarah Sands. The purple lilac on the right is a late Minuet, introduced from Canada. Facing page: A carriage circles the Annex Commons.

Jennifer Wohletz

Swirled old bark
Wind whorled
Time twisted
They say lilac wood
Runs purple at its core

Jennifer Wohletz

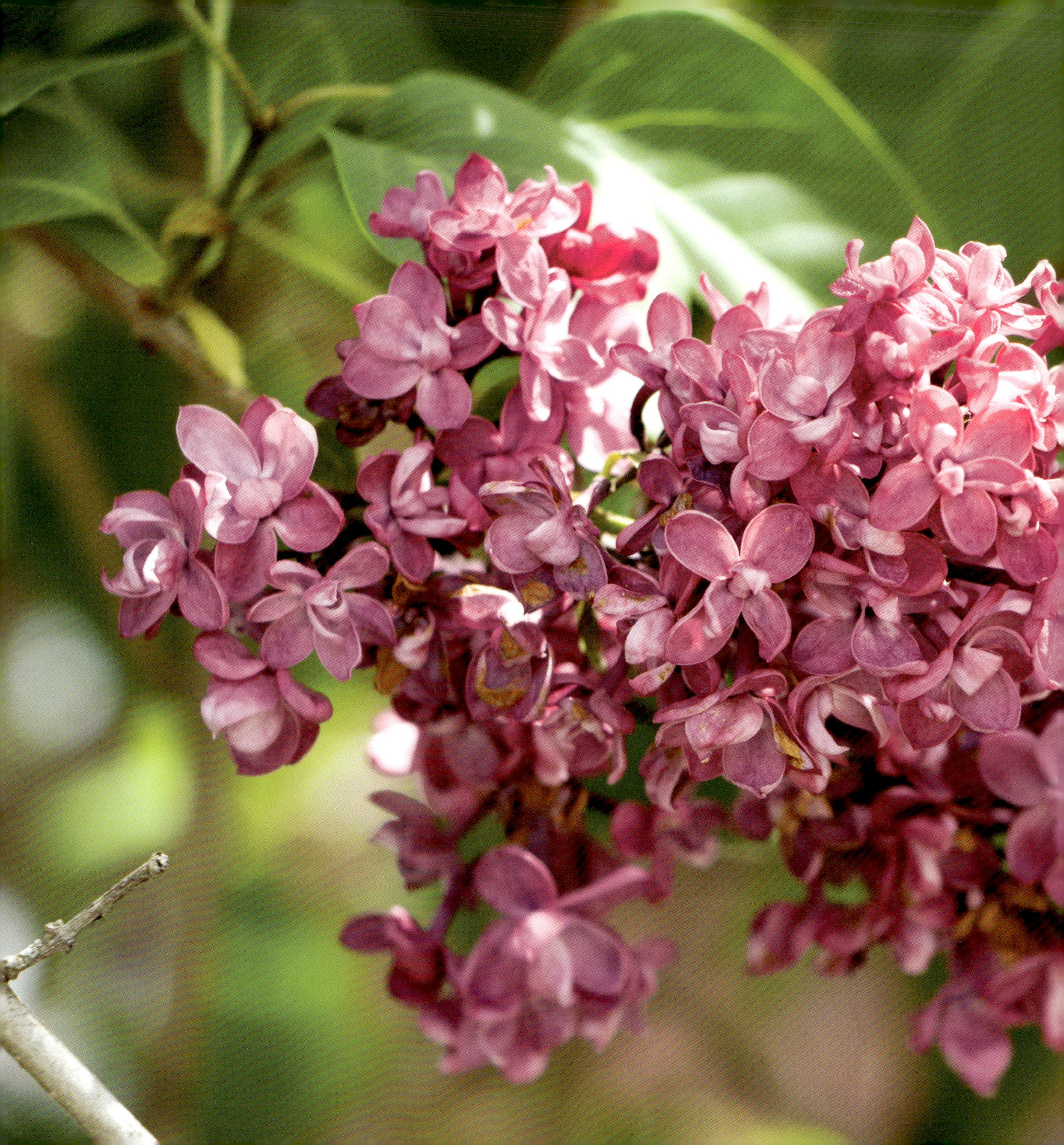

Jennifer Wohletz

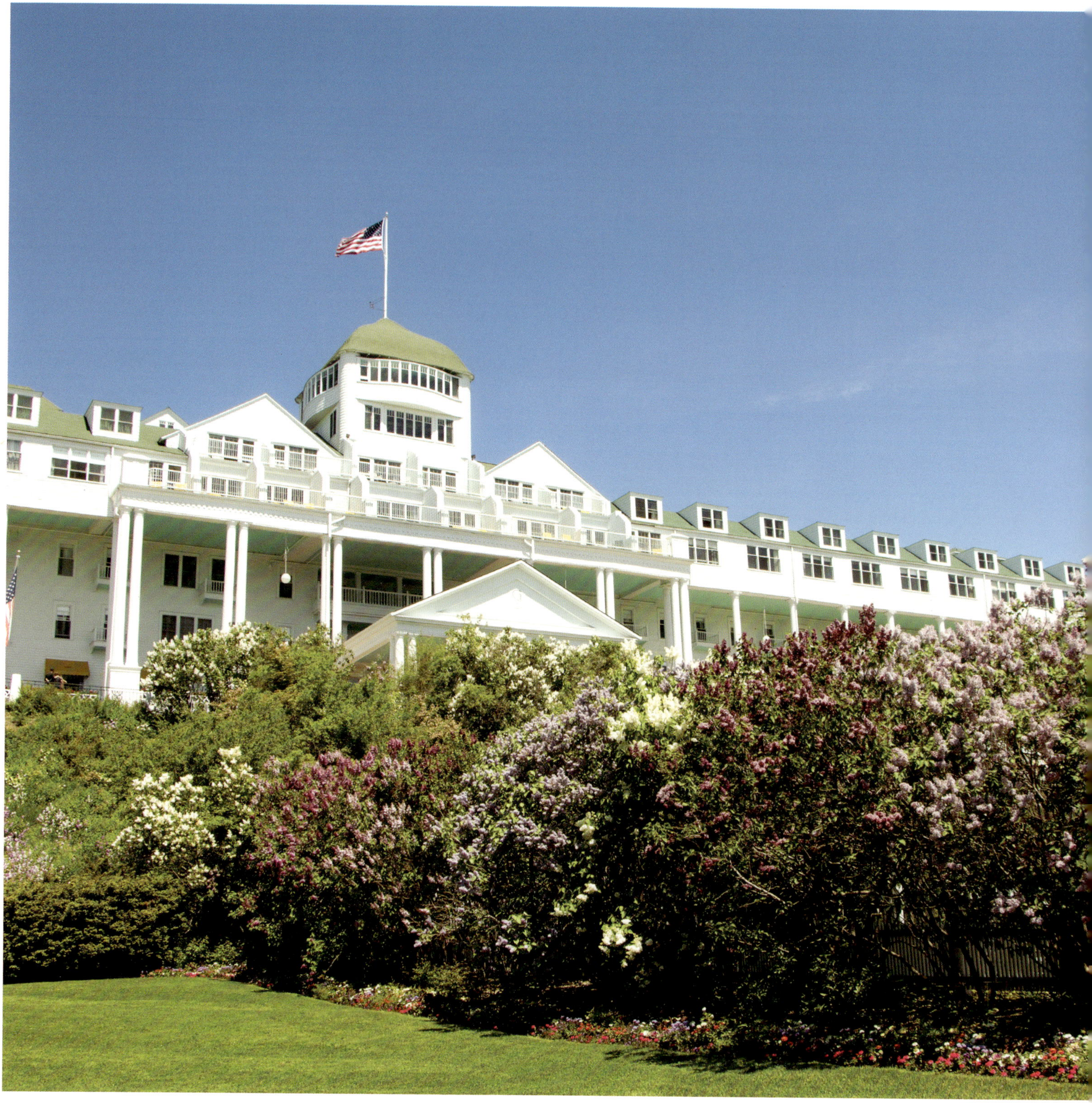

Sara Wright

Sara Wright

Left: This lilac hedge creates a majestic, fragrant foreground by the pool at Grand Hotel. Top: Lilacs and American flags herald the beginning of the summer season at Grand Hotel. Above: A purple canopy rises above a walkway in Grand Hotel's lower gardens.

Jennifer Wohletz

A well-groomed hedge of lilacs lines the fence dividing Grand Hotel's Esther Williams Pool and Tea Garden. A ferry departs the island at sunset. They say people have smelled lilacs from ferries as far away as a mile offshore. Inhale, and enjoy these spectacular blossoms in your imagination.

Sara Wright

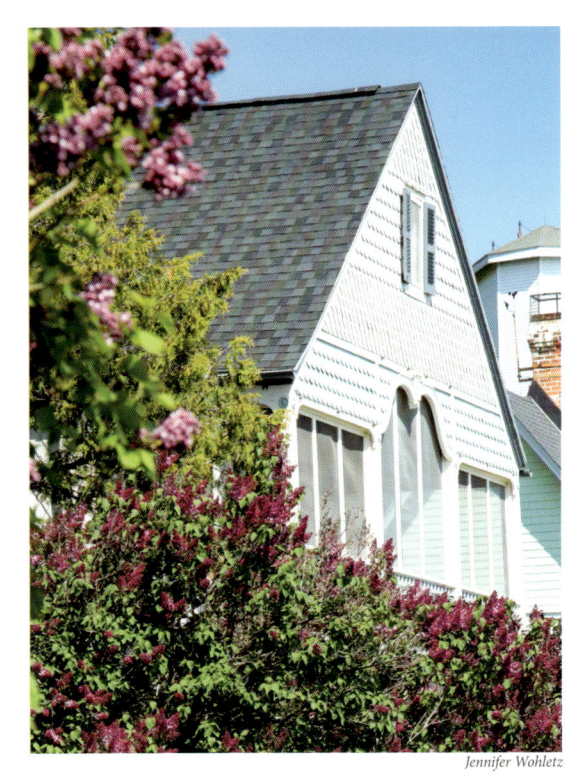

Top: Small foundation lilac shrubs and larger ones in yard balance well. Above left: Magenta and dark pink lilacs make a bold statement. Above right: Straight from the "Gilded Age." Facing page: Opulent pale pink flowers before a backdrop of blooms in varying colors.

Jennifer Wohletz

Tiny palms open
Spraying perfume
All over June

Jennifer Wooletz

Jennifer Wohletz

Jennifer Wohletz

White and purple shrubs planted together create surprise and delight in these West Bluff gardens.

Photo on pages 54-55: The aptly named 'Sensation' (Syringa vulgaris) lilac is the only bi-color lilac on the island, with two different colors completely separated on one petal. 'Sensation' is a very rare bi-color lilac – bi-color meaning there are two distinct layers of DNA, in this case white and purple. Occasionally, a flower will exhibit one color or the other. It originates from Holland in the 1930s when a nurseryman discovered the unusual petals on a lilac named 'Hugo de Vries'.

Jennifer Wohletz

57

Jennifer Wohletz

Facing page: Dark pink buds open as pink flowers in a riot of color on this 'Sweetheart' (Syringa x hyacinthiflora) lilac. It's one of the many hyacinthiflora lilacs, which bloom early and are all very fragrant. They are a hybrid between a common lilac and another species called 'Oblata' from China, a blend of European and Asian lilacs. Above: Perfect proportions of well-tended lilacs and shrubs at this West Bluff cottage.

Jennifer Wohletz

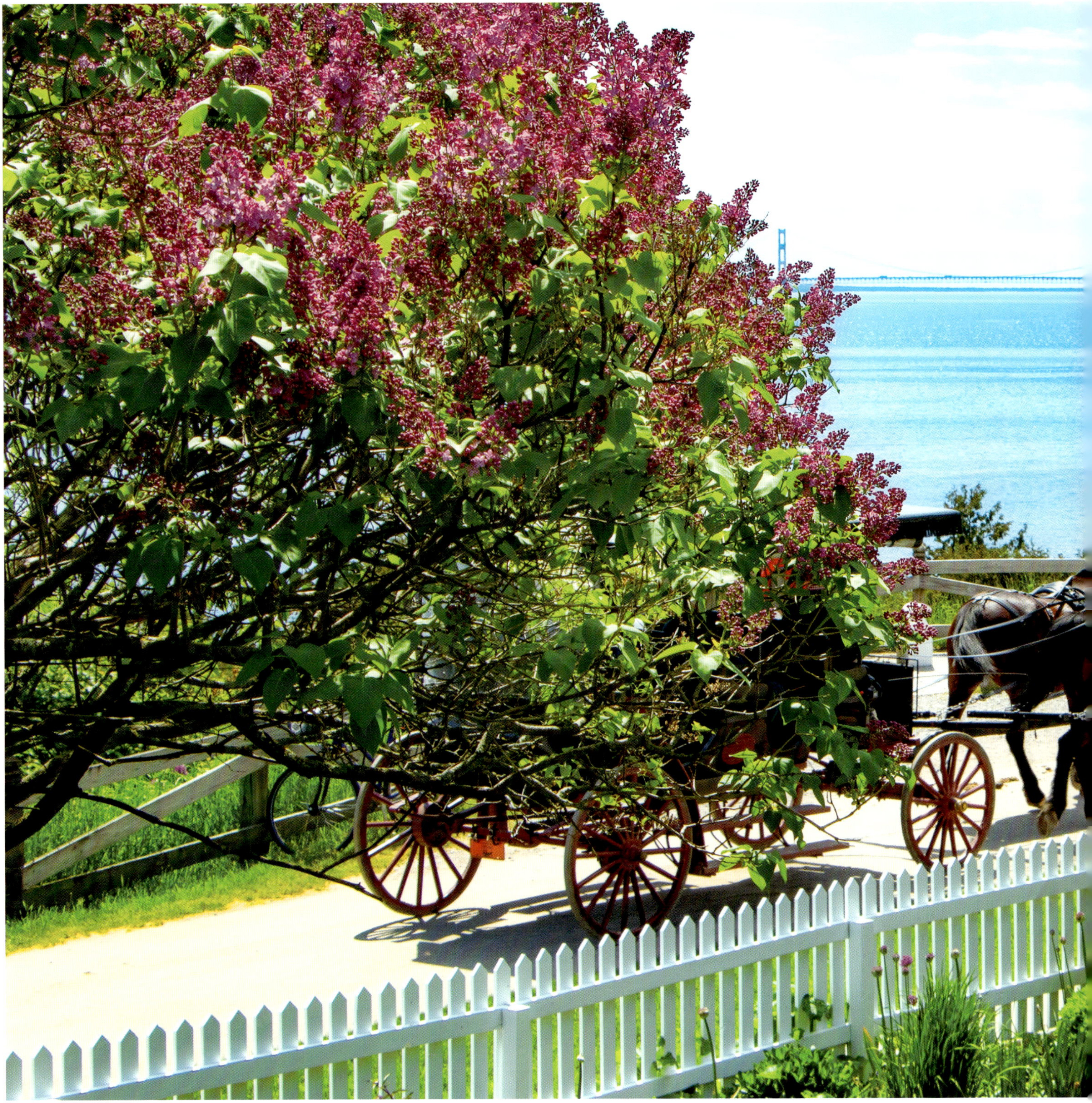

Facing page: A carriage passes an old lilac in the front yard of a West Bluff cottage. Above: The Charles Joly (Syringa vulgaris) lilac is one of Mackinac's finest old French Lilacs. *The large shrub growing wild beyond the Mackinac Island State Park fence on the West Bluff features showy double magenta flowers packed with fragrance.*

A fortnight of fragrance
June jewels of the garden
Lilacs, lilacs, lilacs

Jennifer Wohletz

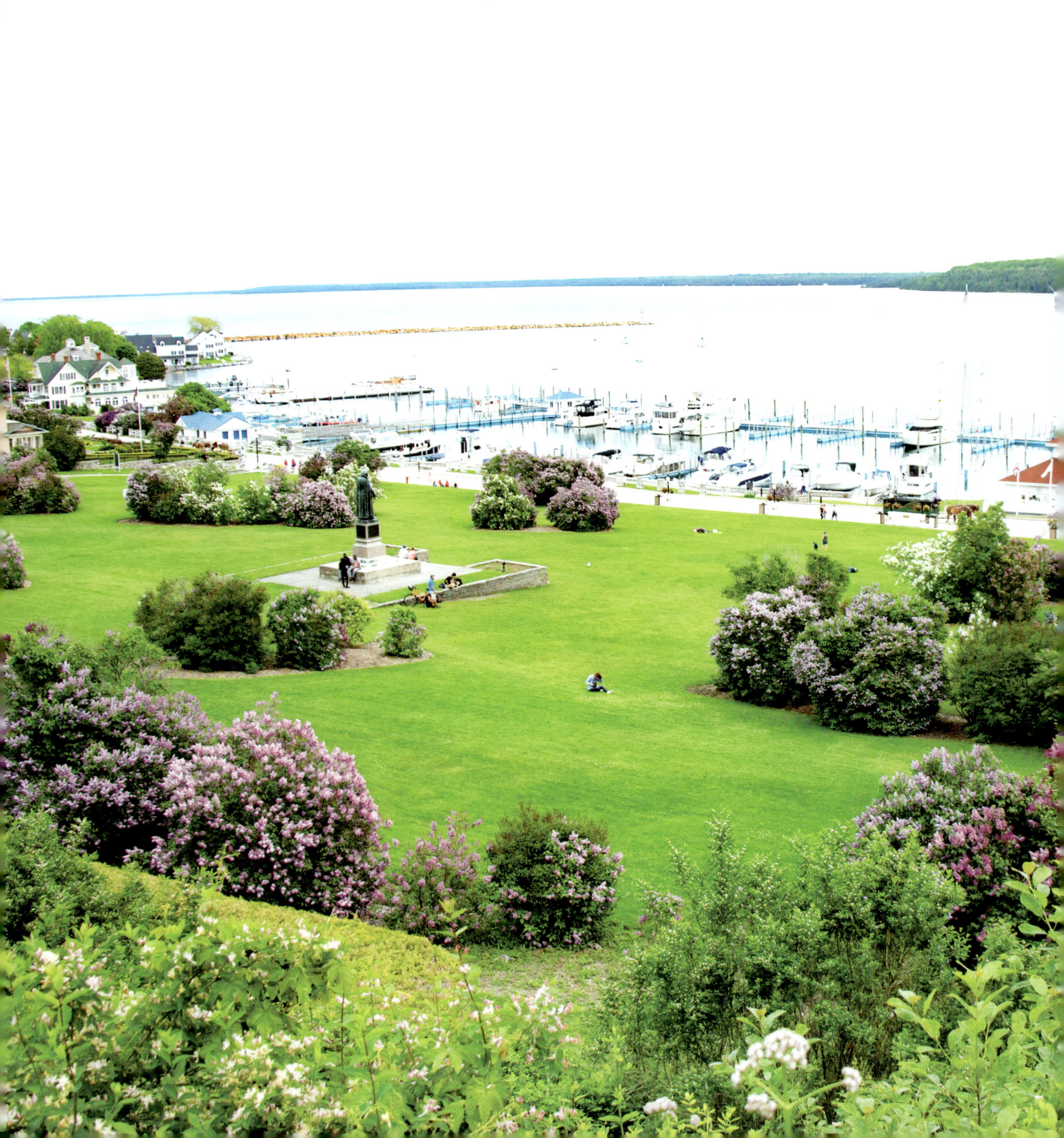

THE BLOOMING BOOMERS

Marquette Park is Home to 75+ Lilac Varieties

If you want to see lots and lots of lilacs, go no farther than Marquette Park, also known as Mackinac's front lawn. You'll be bedazzled by the sheer number and beauty where 115 plants of about 75 different kinds grow in 13 beds. Most were popular post World War II, like the willowy Chinese lilac (*Syringa x chinensis*), the variegated 'Acubaefolia' (*Syringa vulgaris* 'Acubaefolia'), the very early and most fragrant 'Evangeline' (*Syringa x hyacinthiflora* 'Evangeline'), or the Asian beauty 'Miss Kim' (*Syringa pubscens sp patula* 'Miss Kim'). Each lilac brings a difference in color, shape or fragrance.

The first lilac shrubs were planted there by the Mackinac Island State Park Commission between 1904 and 1907, as part of the development of the park. The land had previously served as a vegetable garden for the Fort, and the new park was part of a trend to beautify the island. At that time, the park included curving pathways, flower beds and wooden benches. It was officially dedicated in 1909, when the statue of Jacques Marquette was placed in the center. None of those original shrubs remain. Following World War II and the establishment of the Lilac Festival in 1949, there was a big push to expand Mackinac's lilac population. These baby boomers greatly expanded the park's lilac population. In the early 60s, workers planted new bushes in Marquette Park when the Mackinac Island State Park Commission made a dedicated effort to focus on lilacs. They have thrived for over half a century thanks to Mackinac's cool weather with its breezes and mists – the perfect environment for lilacs to flourish.

continued on page 67

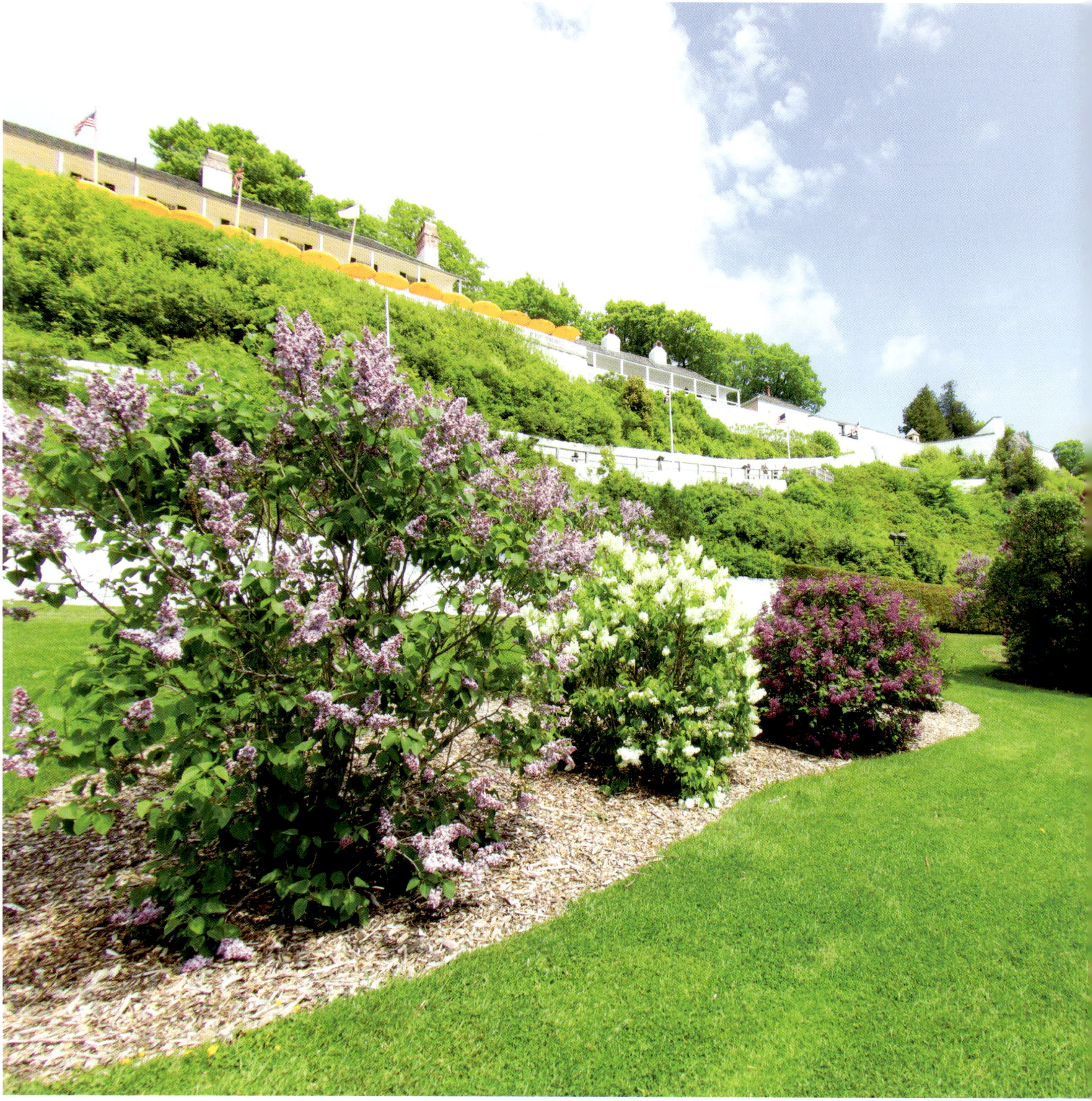

Jennifer Wohletz

Lilacs Need Care to Survive, Thrive

continued from page 65

In the new millennium, things did not go so well for the lilacs. "The problem was that about half of the lilacs were grafted plants and thus the cultivar was not on its own roots. At that time, grafting was a common practice to clone the original cultivar. When the lilacs got into that 50-to 60-year-old range the graft unions started to fail, and without the suckering that an ungrafted lilac would have, there was no way for the plant to regenerate itself," explains lilac expert Jeff Young, who was brought in to examine the aging plants.

"Our first effort was to remove the grafted plants. Almost all were in very poor condition. We removed the dying plants to prevent disease from spreading. Should an infection begin in the old and dying plants, it could easily wipe out the entire planting. Michigan's experience with the Emerald Ash Borer brings home the necessity of maintaining a healthy planting of any kind, especially one so iconic to the island. Our second effort was to revive the plants that were on their own roots. We removed all gardening fabric, enlarged the beds, and added mulch to the soil around the plants. To our delight, the plants responded the next year with great vigor and every one of them suckered and produced many new stems. We allowed this suckering for a few years until the new stems flowered; then we gradually removed the remaining old stems. This has largely proved successful."

continued on page 70

Jennifer Wohletz

Marquette Park: Mackinac Island's Front Yard is Awash with Fragrant Blooms

Jennifer Wohletz

68

Seventy-five+ different kinds of lilacs grow in 13 beds throughout Marquette Park.

Jennifer Wohletz

Gardeners Avoid Pruning the Suckers to Bolster Lilacs in Park

continued from page 67

On Mackinac Island the lilacs love the rocky limestone (high pH) soil, the constant breeze off the lake and the many sunny locations like Marquette Park. They pretty much survive on occasional irrigation but mostly by the rain. To support the well-being of a lilac, expert Jeff Young believes it's good to first think about how the lilac lives in the wild. Their roots come up as new stems a foot or so from the mother stem and thus perpetuate that lilac.

"That's why gardeners who care for the lilacs in Marquette Park do not prune them much. We just remove the old or broken stems that need to be removed," Jeff Young explains. "Also, we don't fertilize them. Instead we add a thin layer of bark mulch to protect them from potential encounters with a string trimmer or lawn mower. The beds in Marquette Park are wide so the soil doesn't get compacted and damage the roots. We let the suckers perpetuate the lilac, annually thinning them to make room for all the stems. Good air circulation means no mildew. We do get after the other nuisance plants that like to grow in beds with the lilacs. We do love diversity, so we are sure to have the lilacs' many siblings, cousins and distant cousins all around.

"When the lilacs do need more attention we depend on people who know them well. Their caregivers are trained, even some friendly Master Gardeners. They use the right tools like a by-pass pruner, nice and sharp. We don't care if the lilac is skinny or fat, tall or short, but is sturdy, balanced and shapely for that Victorian touch. After the flower finally passes, we rarely deadhead. The energy for seeds is much better spent on setting buds for more flowers next spring. But, if it's more flowers you want, as soon as that flower passes, snip it off. Once the flowers have passed, your pruning should all be done. Now let the lilac thrive and grow for that reward in the spring."

Nancy May

Jennifer Wohletz

Jennifer Wohletz

Jennifer Wohletz

Jennifer Wohletz

FATHER JACQVES MARQVETTE
WITH LOVIS JOLIET DISCOVERER
OF THE MISSISSIPPI RIVER
FOVNDER OF THE SAINT IGNACE
AND KASKASKIA MISSIONS
AN EXPLORER ARDENT AND
RESOVRCEFVL · A SHEPHERD
WHO GAVE HIS LIFE FOR
THE SHEEP

More Rumor than Poem

James J. Bogan, Jr.

While the rumor that lilacs were brought to Mackinac Island
by French Jesuits is untrue, the idea still inspires modern day poets.

Not to be found in the Jesuit Relations
is the report from a spring day in 1671
when Père Marquette left the mission in St. Ignace
and paddled over to Big Turtle Island,
Louis Jolliet at the stern stroking two for one.
The priest at the bow surveyed the land
gawking like any latter day fudgie,
but no monstrous buildings distracted
from the greens of the path-wound woods.

His task had appeared to him in a waking dream back in Laon,
a floating St. Fiacre, spade in hand, whispered:
"Jack, lad, plant our French Lilac trees in sacred soil.
You will know the place when you feel it."
Thus the cargo rides amidships in the birchbark canoe,
a batch of thirty-four saplings, one from each province of France,
now splashing towards branched destiny.

After an invocation to St. Fiacre
Marquette instructed Jolliet, spade in hand,
to plant the plants near the Ojibway village on the Island.
After mumbling through his daily Office,
the priest too dug and planted, until all the varieties
of lavender, pink, white, and purple immigrants
were tamped down and watered from the blue bay.

So Père Marquette's statue today oversees
the grove of Lilacs he fathered, call it 350 years ago.
The last words uttered from his death-mat
on the shores of the Notipekago River are said to have been:

"N'oublie pas de bien tailler les lilas de l'île Mackinac ---
mais seulement après qu'ils auront fleuri au printemps."
("Don't forget to prune the Lilacs on Mackinac Island,
but only after they have flowered.")

Jennifer Wohletz

Jennifer Wohletz

Jennifer Wohletz

Allison Sehoyan

Facing page: For whom the bell tolls – today it's for the lilacs. Top left: This 'Katherine Havemeyer' (Syringa vulgaris 'Katherine Havemeyer') French lilac produced by Emile Lemoine in 1922 features large, lightly scented double blooms with heart-shaped foilage. Top right: One bouquet of this fragrant French hybrid can perfume an entire cottage parlor. The 'Beauty of Moscow' (Syringa vulgaris 'Krasavitsa Moskvy') lilac boasts soft pink buds that open to enormous blooms. Left: A steady stream of cyclists enjoy the fragrance of lilacs as they pedal past Marquette Park.

This Chinese lilac called, Purple Haze (Syringa 'Purple Haze'), was planted in the Mackinac Island State Harbor grounds by lilac expert Jeff Young. The lilac was propagated by Young's friend, Jack Alexander of the Arnold Arboretum of Harvard University, who visited the Island in 2007 to see the lilacs.

Jennifer Wohletz

Bill Early planted these lilacs during the summer from 1971 to 1978. "He planted the lilacs all by himself while I was working in the Cannonball," says Cass Early. "Bill had a theory that you had to do them in the fall – he had a theory about everything. We didn't prune them. They were on their own." Today, the home is owned by Ryan Macy, who continues to care for the beautiful hedge lining his yard.

THE 21st CENTURY

Lilacs Add Early Color, Fragrance

Thanks to early plant explorers, breeders, and nurserymen, the selection of lilacs today is like never before. The choices are a botanical smorgasbord. You can choose from dwarf plants to trees and any size in-between; from large panicles with white florets outlined in purple, or purple flowers outlined in white; from early to late bloomers, stretching the typical "fortnight of fragrance" into a month. Blossoms are bigger, fuller, some giant doubles, and the permutations of color a spectrum from deep pink to blue.

A wide variety can be seen in many Mackinac gardens, both public and private. Landscape designer Jack Barnwell says, "Lilacs are an integral part of any Mackinac Island landscape or garden project. Not only do they thrive on the island with very little care, but their signature look, fragrance, and inviting nature make any garden space look right at home on Mackinac."

At the north end of the island, Cass Early and her late husband, Bill created a huge lilac hedge on their property across the street from the Cannonball Drive Inn, a fast-food stop. They owned the eatery from 1971 to the 1990s and Bill is a descendant of the Early family who once farmed the area. "The old lilac tree in the yard was there when we moved in," says Cass. "As far as I know it had always been there. I don't know who planted it or when, but it's very old." Bill took suckers from it and planted them along the fence on British Landing Road. His theory was when you planted the suckers you had to plant all of them in the same direction as when you got them out from the ground. Bill planted them over the years from 1971 to 1978.

Jennifer Wohletz

Sweet Scented Lilacs Trigger Fond Memories of Loved Ones

Gardening author Jennifer Bennett wrote, "Plant a lilac and you plant a memory." For island resident and writer Jean Allen, that is true in a bittersweet way. Her oldest son, Doug, planted a lilac in her front yard on her birthday about 30 years ago. He passed away in 1997. Through the years, the shrub has grown to the second story of her home, Candlelight Cottage. "Every time I look at the tree I think of Doug," says Jean. Doug started the Butterfly House on the island. A horticulturist and nature lover, Jean says her son's spirit is vested in the beautiful lilac, especially when it blooms in June. And when those who planted lilacs are long gone, the memories of their sweet scents and blossoms will live on in future generations.

Jennifer Wohletz

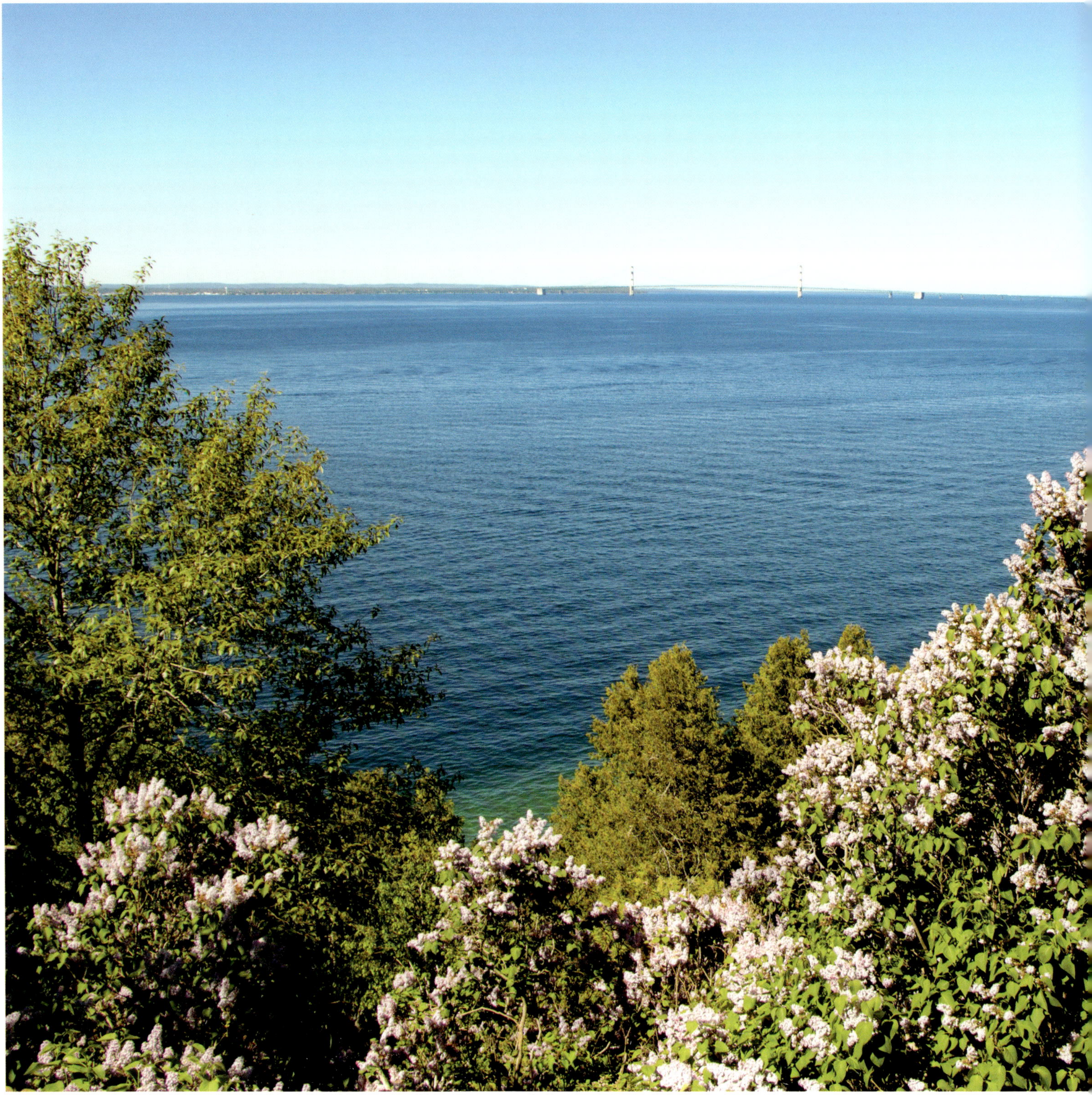

West Bluff View Features Pink Lilacs, The Mackinac Bridge

More than 50 shrubs – many as tall as small trees – grace the tiered hillside behind Hahn Cottage (a.k.a. Lover's Leap Cottage), a white pillared summer home perched on the bluff in Hubbard's Annex. The plants line stone walls and stairs that lead to a tennis court below. The lilacs were already there when owner Sharon Hahn and her husband, Bill, purchased the home in 1987. "The lilacs have spread like beautiful, aromatic weeds," says Sharon Hahn. "I look forward to early June when the scent of lilacs wafts up the bluff and into the open windows of the cottage. There's nothing quite like it."

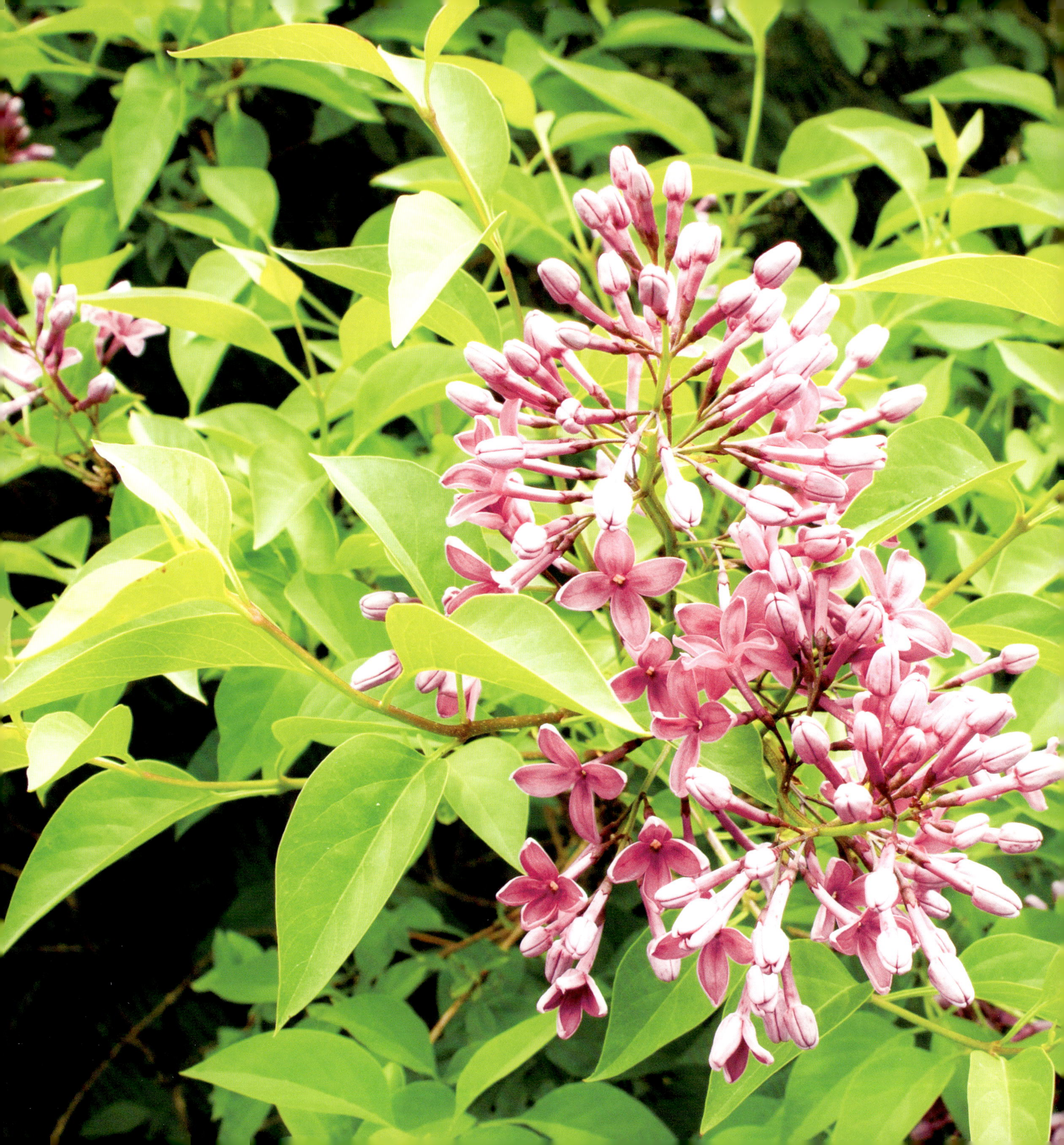

Lilacs

by Jim Lenfestey

Are in the air each spring,
lavender clumps of fragrant
grandmothers dying, dying
as it is written on earth even
in spring, grandmothers in old
photographs with lilac sprigs
at their ears and lilac bundles
under their faces under tumbles
of laughter toward loved ones,
dying now in haunting fragrance
of life abundant, no care now
how soiled and tortured the roots,
how many branches died,
as we shoots, we shoots, we shoots
rise all around, forgiven,
rooted, glorious, ungovernable.

Jennifer Wohletz

Planting a Lilac Commemorates Special Occasions

Over the course of many Lilac Festivals, Lorma Kolatski and her family have accumulated 19 lilac shrubs. Five of them in varying colors, from dark lavender to pink, grace her yard in the village of Harrisonville. The grandmother says, "Four of my lilac bushes were all off of lilac floats in the Lilac Parade from when four of my granddaughters were princesses. Each float had two trees, so I planted one in my yard and the other went to my granddaughters' yards."

The tradition of crowning a Lilac Queen with a court of princesses dates back to 1949. Although Lorma's daughter, Louann Mosley, was Lilac Queen one year, she didn't receive a tree because there wasn't room on the float for one that year. But Louann wasn't upset: her son, Benjamin, has given her a lilac shrub every Mother's Day since he was a little boy, and the tradition continues.

Jennifer Wohletz

Jennifer Wohletz

Jennifer Wohletz

Jennifer Wohletz

Jennifer Wohletz

Facing page: A large lilac shrub in the village of Harrisonville. Top: Yes, there's a house behind that huge lilac tree in Harrisonville. The shrub is from a sucker taken from an old lilac bush on the former Early farm. At 10' wide and 15' tall, it's still growing. Bottom: A dray passes beneath a lilac on Cadotte Avenue.

Jennifer Wohletz

89

Jennifer Wohletz

Above: This Japanese Tree lilac blooms in an East Bluff cottage garden after other lilacs fade on the island. Facing page: Late-blooming Japanese Lilac tree weaves a lacy tapestry against the sky.

Jennifer Wohletz

Jennifer Wohletz

This East Bluff garden features a mix of lilac, perennials, evergreen shrubs and annuals for full-season color. It's a perfect example of how simple single pink lilacs can be properly pruned and used in a landscape. The garden features a variety of different colors, nice proportionality and plants that are well tended.

Jennifer Wohletz

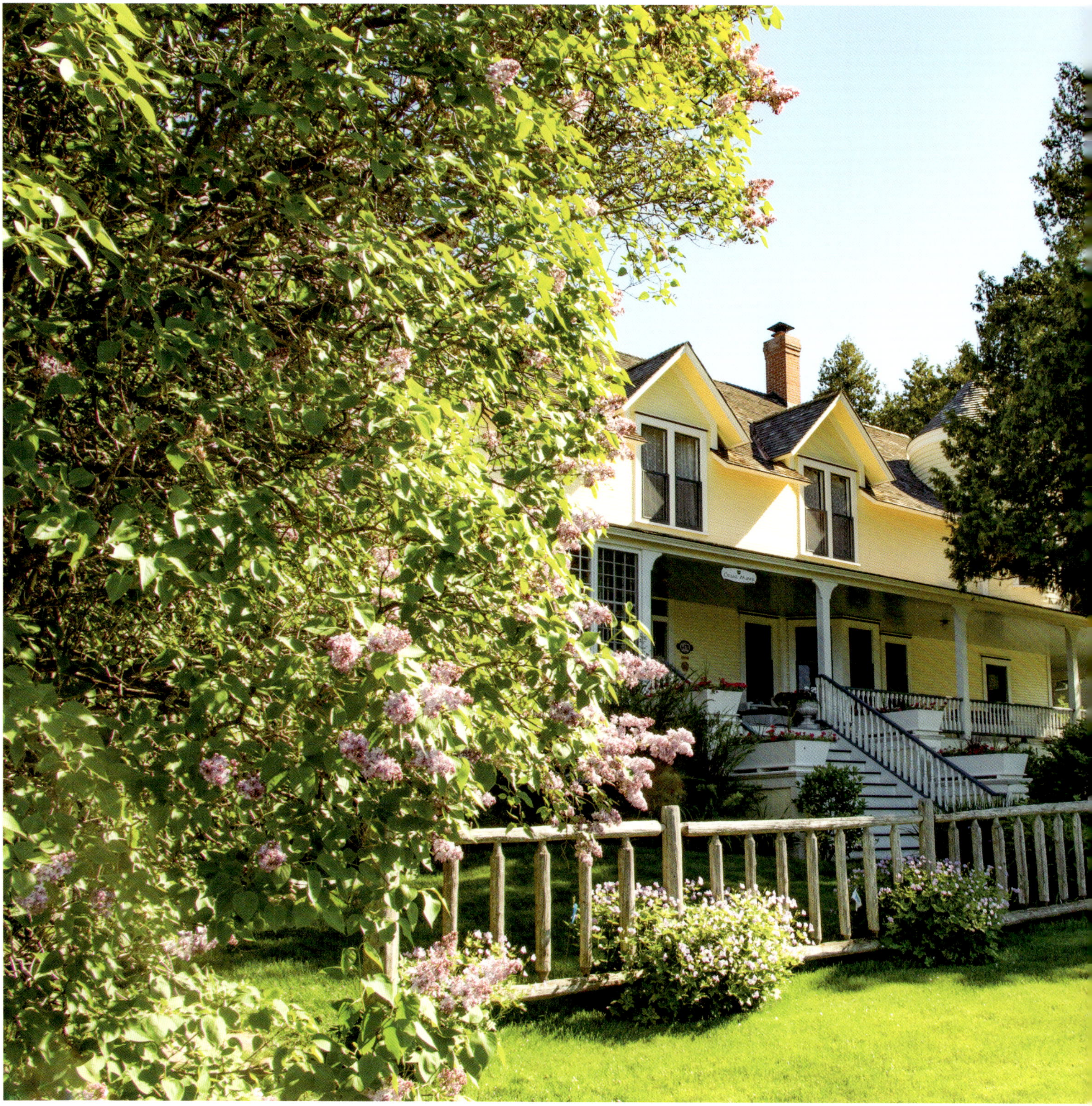

Jennifer Wohletz

Jennifer Wohletz

Jennifer Wohletz

Facing page: From tall to small, lilac shrubs add color and grace to the front view of this East Bluff cottage. Top, above & left: Lilacs rise behind a pergola in the East Bluff cottage's backyard garden and even scent the horse corral.

Jennifer Wohletz

95

Lilacs party in the sun
Horses at work
Look straight ahead

Jennifer Wohletz

Jennifer Wohletz

Jennifer Wohletz

Facing page: A team of Grand Hotel horses high step on their way to pick up passengers. This page: Mackinac Island Carriage Tour guests pass blooming lilacs during the tour. The purple lilacs at Surrrey Hill are called 'Royality' (Syringa x josiflexa 'Royality.')

Jennifer Wohletz

Jennifer Wohletz

Jennifer Wohletz

Jennifer Wohletz

Jennifer Wohletz

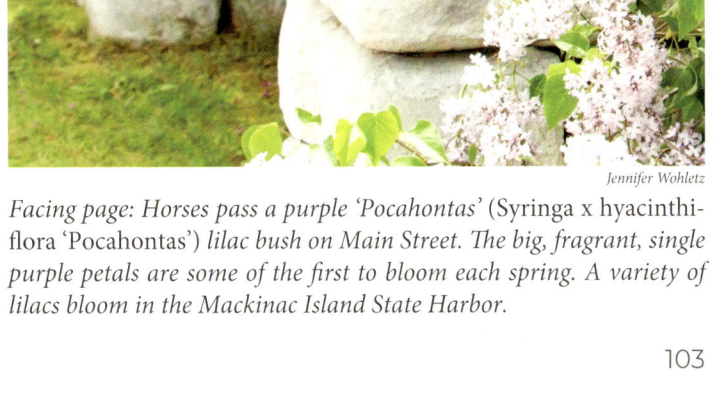

Jennifer Wohletz

Facing page: Horses pass a purple 'Pocahontas' (Syringa x hyacinthiflora 'Pocahontas') lilac bush on Main Street. The big, fragrant, single purple petals are some of the first to bloom each spring. A variety of lilacs bloom in the Mackinac Island State Harbor.

Jennifer Wohletz

Dan Wohletz

Jennifer Wohletz

Left: A Common lilac's petals begin to open before a backdrop of the lake and lighthouse. Top: The International Lilac Society gifted 150 collector plants to Mackinac Island, including the yellow Morton Garden's variety of 'Primrose' and white 'Frederick Olmstead' in this hedge at Windermere Point by the Mackinac Island Public Library. The Society members planted the yellow between the two bright white to show off the yellow petals featuring a tiny yellow stripe. Above & facing page: They also planted the purple 'Etna', which was introduced in 1927.

Jennifer Wohletz

Hard-working horses
Did you not notice
The lilacs waving to you?

Jennifer Wohletz

Jennifer Wohletz

Dale Gallagher of Mackinac Island took care of the Island's cemetery for 36 years. He planted lilacs along this fence line, and some of them spread down the hill onto other lots.

Jennifer Wohletz

Jennifer Wohletz

Jennifer Wohletz

Jennifer Wohletz

Jennifer Wohletz

116

Jennifer Wohletz

Jennifer Wohletz

Jennifer Wohletz

Jennifer Wohletz

Facing page: Some of the island's premier lilacs grow in the church garden, a gift from the International Lilac Society. A view of Ste. Anne's framed by lilacs in Marquette Park. Lilac branches at the Rectory frame Ste. Anne's Catholic Church. Top left & above: This old French lilac called 'President Grevy' falling over the shoulder of the Virgin Mary is one of the original double blues. Top right: an 'Anabel' lilac. Left: A 'Maiden's Blush' lilac.

117

Jennifer Wohletz

Jennifer Wohletz

Jennifer Wohletz

118

Jennifer Wohletz

Mission Point Resort's sprawling 18-acre waterfront property features beautiful gardens exploding with color throughout the season thanks to a vast array of blooming wildflowers, perennials, annuals and lilacs. Plants are added to the The Proven Winner's Signature Garden every year, including new lilac varieties such as 'Beauty of Moscow', 'Yankee Doodle', 'Wonderblue' and 'Primrose'.

Jennifer Wohletz

Jennifer Wohletz

119

Jennifer Wohletz

Above: Better than hay. This horse at Mackinac Island's Little Barn snacks on a common lilac. Did you know lilac flowers are edible? Best consumed in small quantities because they smell better than they taste. Right from top: Lilacs can enhance a landscape in nearly any setting. Here they frame a view of Round Island Lighthouse. In Sunset Forest, lilacs bloom on a terraced hill behind Far, Far Away Cottage. At Metevier Inn, a centenarian lilac in the front yard plays a key role in the landscape, even after the blooms fade. Facing page: The lilac bloom outside a lace curtained cottage window on Bogan Lane is 'Nadezhda' (Syringa vulgaris 'Nadezhda'), one of the most beautiful Russian lilacs.

Joanne Ripple

Jennifer Wohletz

Jennifer Wohletz

Kate Dupre

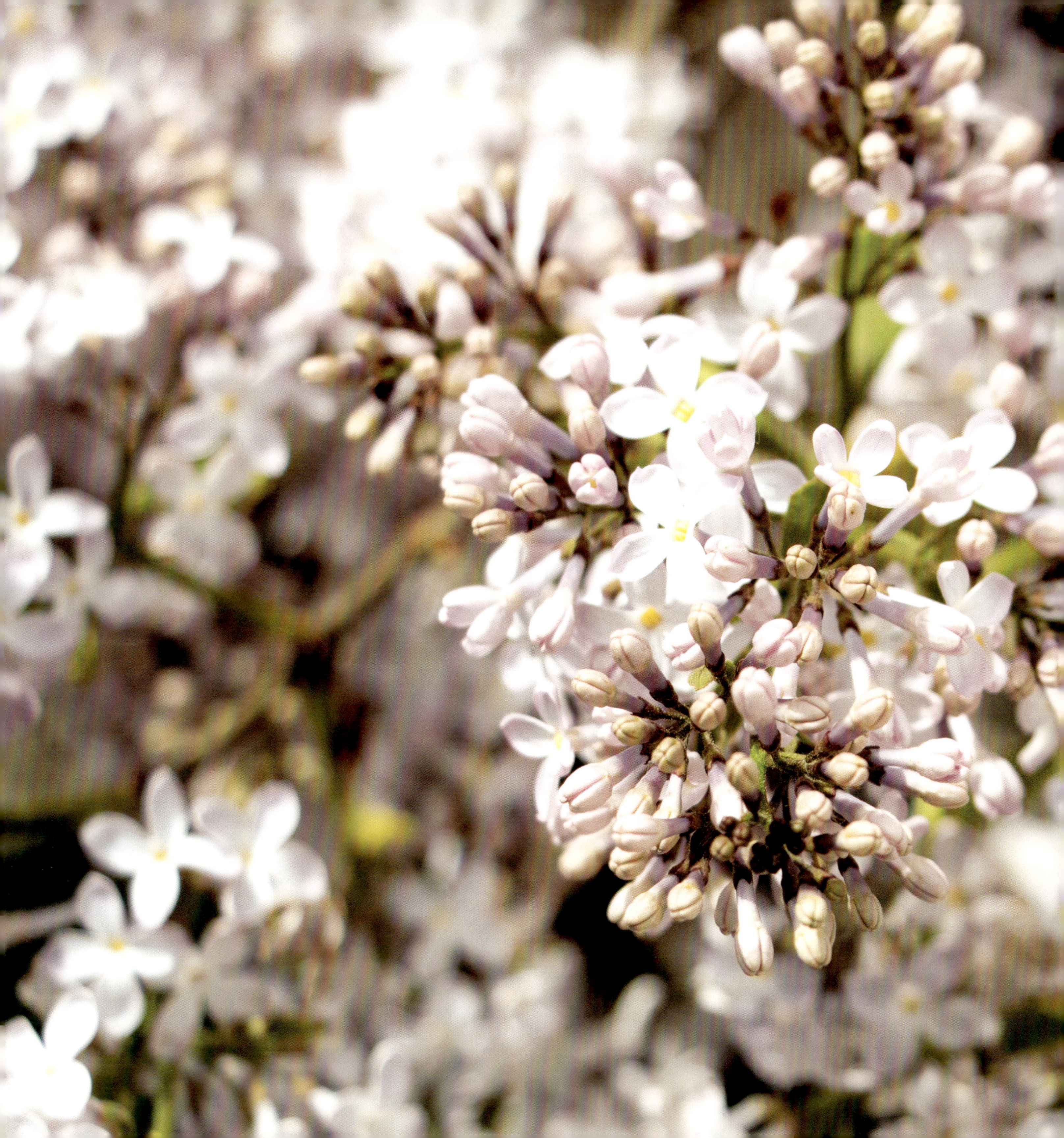

The Lilacs were Late this Year

by Phillip Rice

The lilacs were late this year
and yet the rains seemed to stop for nothing,
not even the meeting of old friends,
not even news of dying friends,
or the news of dead friends
May passed unnoticed, and most of June
And then, suddenly, as if promised
by some thankless prophet
they appeared—glorious purple, pink,
white, with heart-shaped leaves,
moody and tearful, the lilacs
And we were left, wondering
if there is really no death.

Jennifer Wohletz

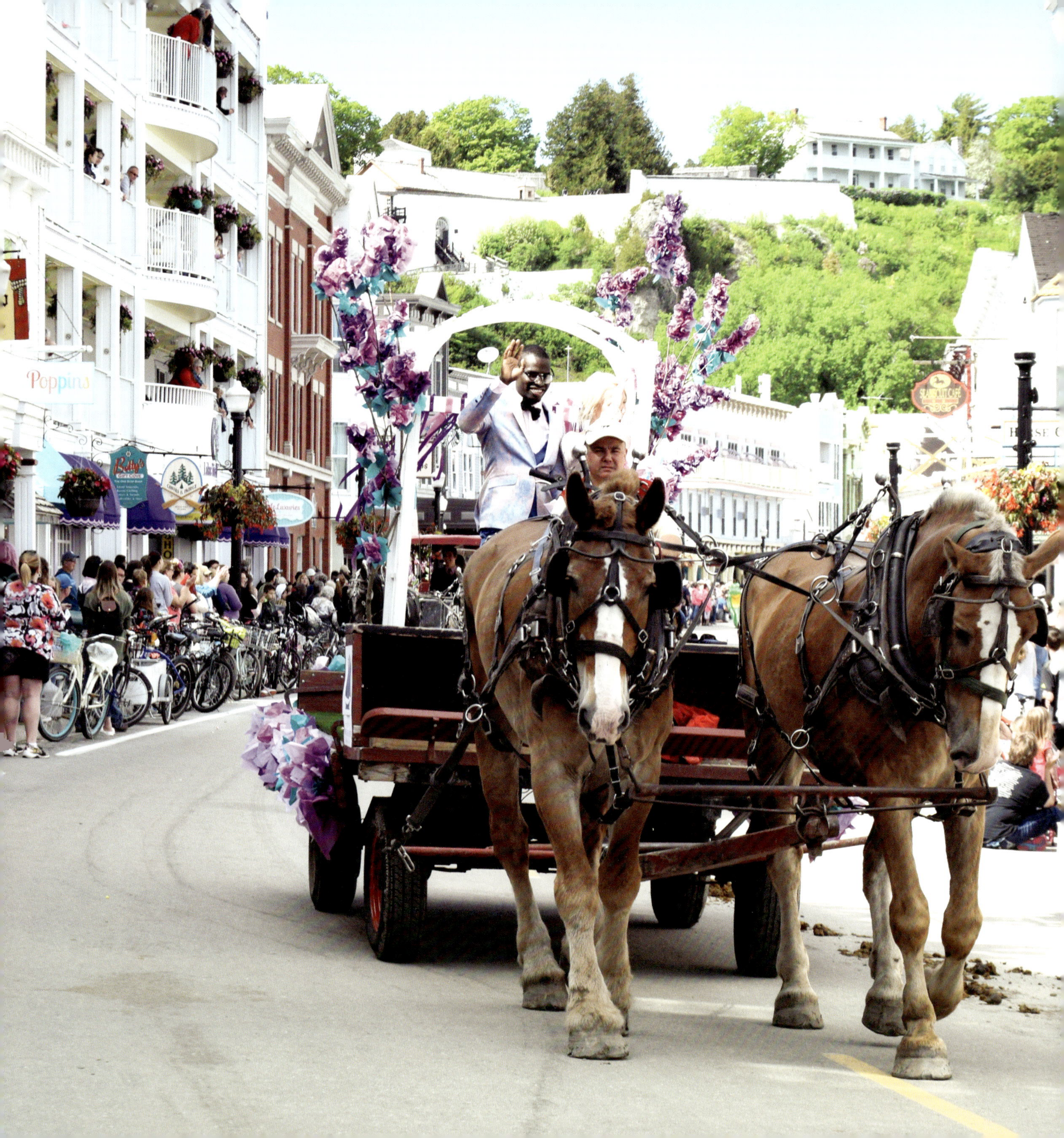
Poppins

THE LILAC FESTIVAL

Mackinac Island Lilac Lovers Celebrate Iconic Flower with Parades & More

The Lilac Festival tradition began more than 70 years ago, the brainchild of two island women, Evangeline "Ling" Horn, who had an antique store on Main Street, and island nurse Stella King. According to the *Island News* (June 20, 1948) "Stella had been dreaming of this parade and planning for it for years, ever since she lived in Washington DC and saw the parades held there at cherry blossom time." It would be fun for local residents, shine a spotlight on the magnificent lilacs, and draw visitors a few weeks earlier than the usual start of the summer season. So, on Sunday, June 20, 1948, Mackinac Island Lilac Day was born.

The first parade was led by the Coast Guard Colors, and Island men in their Marine, Army and Navy uniforms, followed by Mayor Robert Bailey on horseback. Boys rode bicycles with lilac-twined handlebars, while little girls followed them with baskets of lilacs. Sprays of lilacs were sold all along Main Street, and every business on the parade route decorated their windows with lilac displays.

The following year Lilac Day became the Lilac Day Festival, and began the tradition of a Lilac Queen and her court of princesses. Carol Sue Perault (Chambers), then a kindergartener, was crowned Lilac Queen. Governor G. Mennen ("Soapy") Williams came to the island that weekend especially for the Lilac Day Festival, and rode in a carriage in the parade. A cottager sent gigantic balloon figures. "They walked along propelled by a man in each leg and towered over everything," reported the *Island News*.

continued on page 128

The Lilac Man

by Jan Young
avid gardener and wife of Jeff Young, the "Lilac Man"

Eagerly he approaches the object of his
affection, breathing in the sweet
Scent then delicately carrassing her,
enamored of her beauty,
Spring, Summer, Fall and Winter,
each season holds its own
Reason to be drawn to this silent
but majestic lover.

Without words or music he courts her,
Primping, in an attempt
to enhance her natural beauty.
The wind blows and he responds to
her gental movements with
his attention, both growing from
the experience.

Some say beauty is shortlived but he sees
not that fleeting bud,
but the entirety of her existence.

Others may have a passing interest,
seeking enjoyment from
many, but there is but one
love for the Lilac Man.

Jennifer Wohletz

The 2019 & 2020 Lilac Queen, Ava Sehoyan, and her court wave during the 2019 lilac parade. Sehoyan's reign spanned two years due to the Covid-19 global pandemic.

Lilac Queen Reigns Over Festival

The selection of a Lilac Queen has been a highlight of the Lilac Festival tradition since 1949. Then, a police booth where the Taxi Stand is today on Main Street at the coal dock, was used to post photographs of the candidates for queen, and the public selected the winner. The first queen was Sue Perrault (Chambers). She was just six years old when she was coronated as Mackinac Island's first Lilac Queen.

"Stella King started the tradition," recalls Chambers. "She picked me. My dress was made of lavender crepe paper and I wore a fresh lilac crown. We rode on a float, but I don't remember much more. It was scary since I was so young, but now I feel honored to be the first Lilac Queen. It's a great tradition for the island." One of her duties was helping fire the cannon at Fort Mackinac to open the fort for the season. Only one year – 1955 – was the queen not an islander. No one knows for certain, but word has it that the queen was a guest at the Grand Hotel and was chosen by other hotel guests since there was no process for selecting one that year.

Today, the Lilac Queen is a Mackinac Island Public School student selected by a panel of judges and chosen based on an interview process, community involvement and teacher input. It is to honor the student who has dedicated their time to their classmates and community events throughout the year. Generally, the candidates are juniors or seniors. The Lilac Princess is an elementary student chosen by a drawing that takes place at school. Duties include opening Fort Mackinac, riding in the Lilac Festival Parade, and making appearances at many community events for the year of their reign. The history of the festival is featured in a special exhibit at the Stuart House Museum on Market Street. Old and new photographs share visions of former queens and parade floats, while giving visitors a glimpse of how the festival has evolved over the years.

Jennifer Wohletz

"June at the Grand" - linoleum block print by Natalia Wohletz

Artists Capture the Essence of Mackinac Island in Bloom

Lilacs deeply affect many people, not only for their iconic beauty and magnificent colors, but also for their heady and enveloping aroma. They have inspired island artists since the first shrub was planted in the 1800s. Thanks to artists, the essence of lilacs has been captured throughout the years for all to enjoy. Printmaker and summer resident, Natalia Wohletz, says carving the details of "June at the Grand" (above) was a therapeutic creative outlet in 2020. "It was a way to relax and connect with my favorite place, Mackinac Island, during the pandemic stay home order," Wohletz explains. Oil painter and lifelong summer resident, Maeve Croghan, grew up having Mackinac lilacs in her life and hopes to relay their splendor in her paintings. "Lilac Time," (right) captures lilacs growing along the shore road. "The two beautiful old lilacs growing between the boardwalk and shoreline are captivating. Their twisty shapes convey their interesting lives with the Round Island just beyond," says Croghan.

"Lilac Time" – oil painting by Maeve Croghan

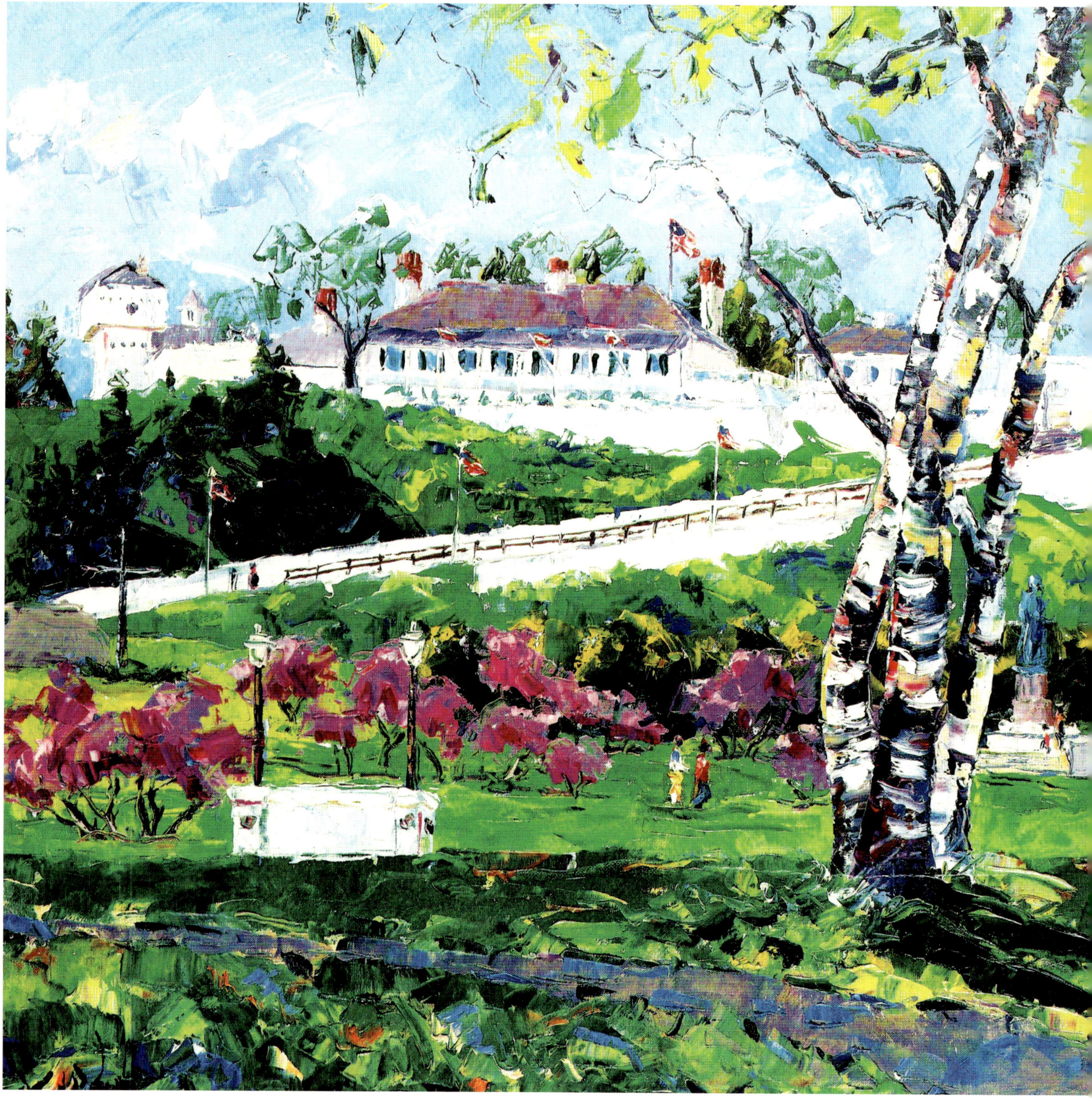

1994 | by Richard Wolfgang

1995 | by Richard Wolfgang

1996 | by Richard Wolfgang

1993 | by Marlee Brown

Annual Lilac Festival Poster Art Contest Celebrates Iconic Blooms

To share work created by lilac-loving aritsts, the Mackinac Island Tourism Bureau (MITB) hosts an annual art contest to select a piece for the official Mackinac Island Lilac Festival Art Poster, which is sold in stores owned by MITB members. The first poster featured a painting of lilacs in Marquette Park with Fort Mackinac in the background by island resident Marlee Brown in 1993. It was sold in limited edition.

Ever since the first official poster in 1993, there has been a new one each year celebrating the iconic blooms. In 1994, the then-Chamber of Commerce members asked Richard Wolfgang, an art instructor and island artist, to create a poster. "It was a huge success," recalls Wolfgang's daughter and island resident, Nancy Chambers. "That 1994 poster was one of Dad's top three. My dad had a great way of capturing the feeling of Mackinac. He thought that what made Mackinac different was the flowers, especially the lilacs. He liked the relationship of the flowers to the water. Every winter after that we had a big family discussion about what he should do for the new poster. It got to be a little stressful in a lighthearted way."

Beginning in 1995, the poster became a competition and Wolfgang won every year until 2007, with the exception of 1998 when artist Joe Cilluffo took the prize for his depiction of a tour carriage passing lilacs blooming on the West Bluff. "My dad stepped aside in 2008 to give other artists a chance," explains Chambers.

Each year artists are asked to submit art on a theme determined by the Tourism Bureau. Artists have free rein, with the only requirement being their work must reflect the theme, and, of course, feature lilacs. The 16" by 20" posters are extremely popular, and a few folks own every one dating back to 1993. Now that's a lot of wall space.

1997 | by Richard Wolfgang

1998 | by Joe Cilluffo

1999 | by Richard Wolfgang

2000 | by Richard Wolfgang

2005 | by Richard Wolfgang

2006 | by Richard Wolfgang

2007 | by Richard Wolfgang

2008 | by Betty Bea Washburn

2013 | by Noel Skiba

2014 | by Diane Neyer

2015 | by Noel Skiba

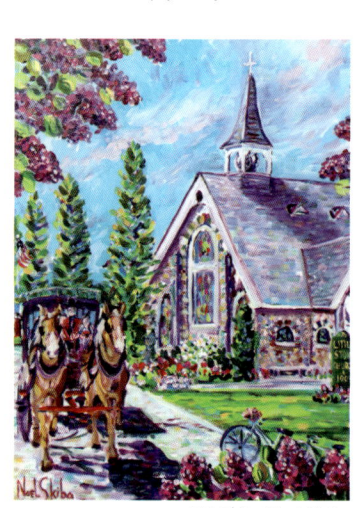

2016 | by Noel Skiba

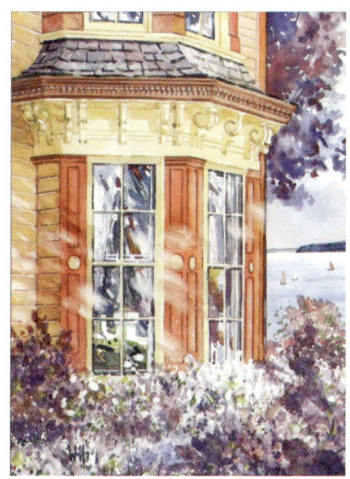

2001 | by Richard Wolfgang

2002 | by Richard Wolfgang

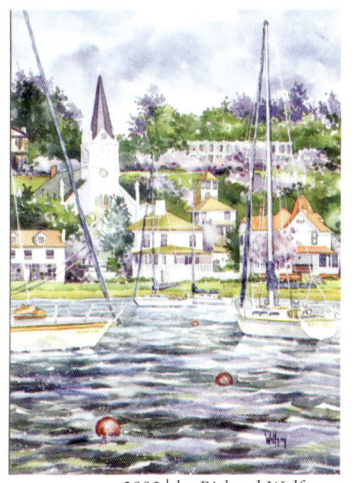

2003 | by Richard Wolfgang

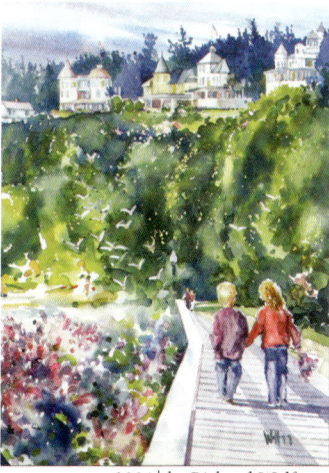

2004 | by Richard Wolfgang

2009 | by Diane Neyer

2010 | by Noel Skiba

2011 | by Kevin Barton

2012 | by Kevin Barton

2017 | by Kevin Barton

2018 | by Kevin Barton

2019 | by Jimmy Taylor

2020 | by JC Demers

Round Island light
Water, sky and shore
Purple lace matting

Jennifer Wohletz

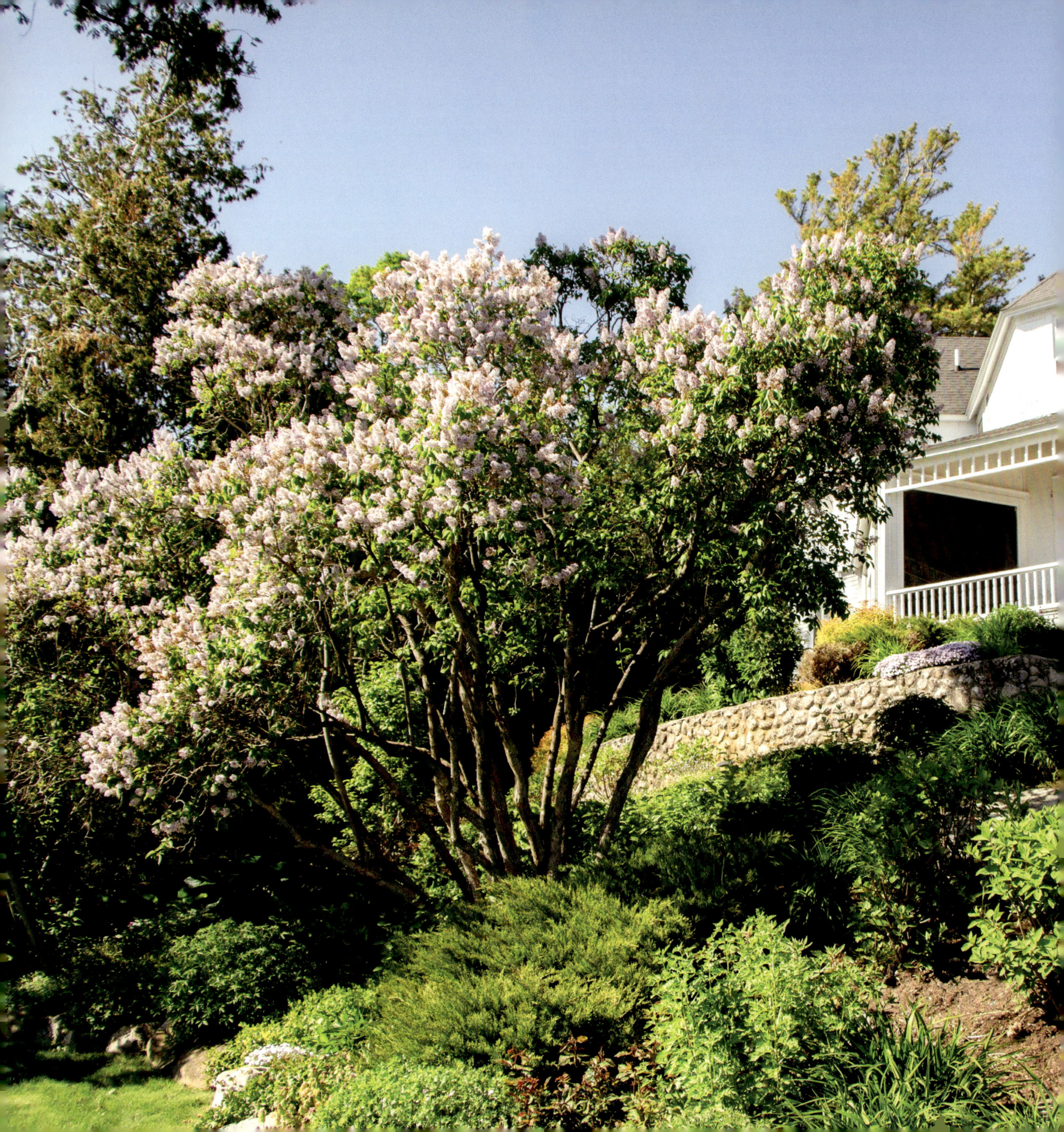

The Future of Mackinac's Lilacs

Tough, Hardy Lilacs Require Care to Stay Healthy, Grow for Generations

Although tough and hardy, lilacs are not immune from the perils of disease, pests, climate change, and human activity. With so many lilacs in one place, a pest like the lilac borer, which lays its eggs on lilac stems and the larvae bore into the wood, could wipe out the island's lilac treasure chest. Excessive ice, rain or drought could also weaken the plant.

"The best defense is to maintain healthy plants," notes lilac expert Jeff Young. That incudes proper pruning and removal of dead or diseased stems. Another danger to lilacs is lawn mowers and weedwhackers. Blades and string can knock off bark which may result in death of stems and the ultimate demise of the plant. Creating large planting beds and learning how to properly mow and weed around plants is also helpful.

Mackinac's lilac population has grown and thrived over two centuries, finding a home on this small, rocky island. With over 250 kinds of lilacs, and a few new ones added ever year, these gems of June may continue to flourish with the help of vigilant gardeners and funding. The Mackinac Island Tourism Bureau's Lilac Preservation Fund will help ensure the health of the huge lilac family for generations to come.

The lilac loves the island as much as the islanders love it.

How Not to Prune a Lilac

by Sue Allen

You most common, common lilac
Not a touch of lavender or pink within you,
Just creamy white panicles reaching toward the sky
Though you perfumed our Junes,
you blocked our view of the water
We concluded it was time to cut you down a notch
Not with a pair of pruners, but the executioner's tool

The axe whooshed down
Severing your multiple heads,
a green Medusa with heart-shaped hair

Carting the branches away, the lawn littered in your leaves
We rubbed our hands together, satisfied, hung up the axe
Farewell old white lilac

But you thought only of resurrection
Even beneath the long winter snow
When the frost blew out,
May revealed shoots emerging from your stump,
Green hands waving
Hi there, I'm back!
Surrounded by a skirt of suckers
pushing, poking through the rocky soil
making a mess with your stubborn insistence on life

You win, old warrior
Grow and grow, take the place over
If not our love, you've earned our respect.

Jennifer Wohletz

Tips to Nurture Healthy Lilacs

Whether it's a large ornamental landscape like Mackinac Island's Marquette Park or a small private garden, maintenance is labor intensive. The following are a few tips for nurturing healthy lilacs:

1. Buy small plants. The smaller the plant, the more likely it will live a long life.
2. Avoid buying root bound plants.
3. Plant in full sun.
4. Give them air! They need the breeze so do not overcrowd the planting bed.
5. Leave plenty of room especially near buildings or walls when planting.
6. Practice good pruning technique. Learn how to root prune and plant the bare root method to encourage the growth of feeder roots. Do not use shears or hedge clippers as pruners, which cause lasting damage.
7. Remove old stems to control height and disease.
8. Prune for structure first, then balance, then shape, allowing one or two suckers to mature each year.
9. Avoid over watering, lilacs don't like wet feet.
10. Be careful with the string trimmer and lawn mower.
11. Avoid footpaths or heavy riding lawn mowers near the drip line.
12. Limit the fertilizer, very little is needed. Keep the pH up! Add lime if necessary.

Jennifer Wohletz

Jennifer Wohletz

Above: Lilacs grow over an arbor in a cottage garden on Forest Ridge Road. Facing page: Lilacs make great cut flowers for vases like this arrangement displayed in the front window of Crane Cottage.

Stephanie Crane
147

Sara Wright

Jennifer Wohletz

Jennifer Wohletz

Jennifer Wohletz

Jennifer Wohletz

Facing page: In spring, a wall of lavender, in winter, a palace of ice. The huge lilac hedge near British Landing changes dramatically with each season. Top left & above: Buds form on lilacs in Marquette Park. Bottom left: The West Bluff historic cottages look regal as they patiently await spring and the return of visitors and the fragrant, colorful blooms of lilacs.

About Sue Allen
Author

Writer and teacher, Sue Allen is a lifelong summer resident of Mackinac Island. Some of the common lilacs at her 130-year-old family cottage, Ingleneuk, are out of control, but she is happy to accommodate them. She has a BA in English from the University of Michigan and an MA in Communications from the University of Wisconsin-Superior. Her Mackinac-based fiction novel, *Water Beyond the Bridge*, was published in 2016. She is also co-author of *The Gardens of Mackinac Island*, a coffee table book featuring photographic tours and insightful text about the island's cottage, hotel and public gardens. She owes all she knows about lilacs to Jeff Young, the wise and kindly Lilac Man.

About Jeff Young
"The Lilac Man"

On Mackinac Island, master gardener Jeff Young is known as "The Lilac Man," thanks to his role as the plant specialist for the island's Lilac Festival for more than 16 years. He has taught thousands of visitors about lilacs during Lilac Festival "walk-and-talks" and shared his vast knowledge with Sue Allen for this book. Jeff is a former board member of the International Lilac Society, curator of the lilac collection and horticulature workshop instructor at the University of Vermont Horticulture Research and Education Center. In addition, he has served on the State Advisory Board of the Vermont Master Gardeners, the Board of The Friends of the Hort Farm, the Vermont State Urban Forestry Council, and St. Albans Parks Commission, where he was chairman for nine years. Jeff was a Vermont Master Gardener of the Year in 2007 and awarded senior status (1,000 hours of service) in 2009.

About Jennifer Wohletz Photographer

Photographer Jennifer Wohletz has called Mackinac Island her summer home since 2006. A Michigan State University graduate and certified master gardener, Jennifer has learned so much more about lilac varieties from the Lilac Man and while exploring the island's iconic flowers from behind a camera lens. She hopes to apply this knowledge to nurture the lilacs in her wild garden on the edge of Mackinac Island's Sunset Forest. Jennifer serves on the board of the Mackinac Arts Council and is the co-owner of Main Street Art, a fine art gallery and custom frame shop in Milford, Mich. She loves to share Mackinac stories with island enthusiasts when they visit the gallery. See more of her Mackinac Island-inspired books and photographs wherever books are sold on the island, in Main Street Art's gallery and/or at mackinacislandmemories.com.

About the Contributing Photographers

Creating this book was like building a beautiful lilac puzzle. The following photographers contributed the missing pieces to this photo essay. Stephanie Crane is a life-long summer resident known for her beautiful bouquets of Mackinac lilacs and hydrangeas. Photographer Kate Dupre is also a painter and the owner of Mackinac Island's Watercolor Cafe. Nancy May is a lifelong island resident and accomplished photographer popular for her island images. Joanne Ripple enjoys visiting Mackinac and sharing her island photographs. Allison Sehoyan is an island resident known for her award-winning freighter photographs. Jimmy Taylor is a frequent visitor and award-winning painter and photographer. Dan Wohletz is an island summer resident with a great eye for composition. Sara Wright is an island resident and professional portrait photographer as well as social media specialist.

Mackinac Island Tourism Bureau collection

Bibliography

Sources Cited for *LILACS – A Fortnight of Fragrance on Mackinac Island*

Barnwell, Jack, email correspondence, 02/17/2020

Bennett, Jennifer. Lilacs in the Garden, Firefly Books, 2002, Buffalo, NY.

Beneath the Lilac Canopy (©2016)

Brisson, Steve C., "A Noble Figure: The Story of the Marquette Statues." Mackinac History: A continuing series of Illustrated Vignettes III, no. 4 (2000); email correspondence, 10/11/2019

Chambers, Nancy, interview, 08/02/2019; email correspondence, 11/17/2019

Croghan, Maeve, email correspondence, 03/10/2020

Darga, Doug, email correspondence, 03/18/2020

Dean, Michelle, interview, 10/20/2019

Early, Cass, phone interview, 10/10/2019

Fiala, John L. and Vrugtman, Freek. Lilacs, A Gardener's Encyclopedia, Timber Press Inc., 2008, Portland OR

Fox, Elizabeth, email correspondence, 10/30/2019

Gallagher, Dale, phone call, 10/17/2019

Hahn, Karen, interview

Hygh, Tim, Mackinac Island Tourism Bureau, interview 08/2019

Kolatski, Lorma, interviews, 08/2019, 10/20/2019

www.makinacislandlilacfestival-blogspot.com, accessed 07/30/2019

www.mackinacisland.org

https://en.wikipedia.org/wiki/Lilac_Festival_(Mackinac_Island);accessed 08/05/2019

Macy, Ryan, interview, 03/19/2010

Mauer, Wes, Mackinac Island Town Crier, email correspondence, 01/26/2020

Murray, Steve, phone call, 10/20/2019

Nyer, Diane, interview, 10/02/2019

Porter, Phil, phone call 03/26/2020; email correspondence, 06/27/2019

Slevin, McGuire, Mary, interview 07/15/2019

The Island News, 06/20/1948

Thoreau reference, www.mackinacislandnews.com/news/2013-08-09/News/Thoreau_Scholar_Explores_Authors_Mackinac_Island_W.html

www.mackinacislandnews.com/news/2010-06-10/Top_News/Gardeners_Coloring_Mackinac_With_Thousands_of_Bloo.html

www.mackinacparks.com/mackinac-island-peace-garden/, accessed 10/2019

Yoder, Lydia, email correspondence 02/26/2020;phone interview 03/16/2020

"50th Anniversary of the Mackinac Island Lilac Festival," American Folklife Center, accessed 07/10/2019

POETRY

Allen, Sue; Bogan, Jim; Lenfestey, Jim; Rice, Philip; Young, Glen; Young, Jan Young

HAIKU

Allen, Sue

Jennifer Wohletz